THE MISSING YEARS

Shirley Chau-Zarecki

Dedicated to my parents, my sister and my brother.

Table of Contents

1............4
   The boys 5
   Roller coaster___7
   Mash everything_____9
   The school_____10
   The girls 12
   September 12, 1979____16
   The school year 18
   Half term 22
   Christmas_____25
   Trips_____26
   February 21, 1981_____28
   March 16, 1981_ 30
   Form five 32
   May 15, 1981___34
   September 9, 1981_____36
   Summer job_____38
   November 3, 1981_____40
   Form six_ 42
2_____45
   First day in Wisconsin 46
   June 11, 1982____48
   Host family_____50
   Lakeshore dorm 52
   August 8, 1982_ 54
   Ken_____56
   Trip east_ 58
   First love 61

October 1, 1982 63
First breakup 65
3 67
Summer 1983 Part 1 68
June 20, 1983 69
Summer 1983 Part 2 71
Fall 1983 72
Bei 74
Summer 1984 Part 1 78
First essay 80
Third essay 82
A vent 85
Summer 1984 Part 2 88
September 29, 1984 89
Christmas 1985 91
Bye Bei 94
July 1, 1985 95
Free 97
4 99
The lab 100
No call 102
First date 103
Beauti-asians 105
You've got mail 106
Second date 107
Halloween 109
November 6, 1985 111
Fun and games 113
November 11, 1985 116
Middle child 119
Thanksgiving 120
Christmas 123
True love 124
5 125
First lies 126
Fast forward 128
A snapshot 130
The wedding 131
First pregnancy 134
September 23, 1990 135

Nataja ____ 137
Parker ____ 141
April 26, 1992 ___ 142
The break away 145
Fai _____ 146
Bath _____ 148
A journal entry_ 150
Travis ____ 151
6 _____ 152
Heavy burden __ 153
December 16, 2005 _____ 154
June 17, 2007 ____ 158
Cooking_ 160
Sometime in 2012 _____ 161
True love_ 162

1

The boys

The boys. We referred to them as Gege, meaning older brothers. There were three of them, Kenny, Ben, and Sam, all from Hong Kong. Kenny was round all around, round face, small eyes behind thick round glasses, full black hair forming a new moon over his head, his body was short and a little round in the middle. Ben was the good-looking one, taller, leaner with a no-pimple, every-feature-at-the-right-place kind of face and short straight hair. Sam, well Sam was just Sam, sort of the middle child in my mind, can't remember much about him. But he is absolutely necessary. Without him, it's like a table with only two legs. Besides, there were three of us girls.

The boys were Maria's family friends. They had picked us up at the airport. I learned they were in college, owned their own car, with their own rented house. As far as I know, they were not related, just three college students sharing a house. We were three high school girls with nothing but a large suitcase each. My friend Maria Chen was barely sixteen. My sister Min just turned fifteen. I was sixteen going on seventeen.

Their house was a reddish brown two-story brick box in a line of similar boxes on a quiet street in a suburb of Birmingham. The first night there, the silence hurt my ears. In Hong Kong there were always cars honking, buses buzzing, construction drills whirring, hawkers shouting peddling their ware, kids playing and giggling.

Gege cooked Chinese food. Maria chipped in sometimes. She was a good cook. Min, with her baby face and easy smile, were Geges' favorite. They love to make her smile.

"Do you want to go to the amusement park?" Kenny asked Min one day. She broke out a smile and nodded.

"Yeah!" Maria said.

I watched Ben's silhouette against the kitchen window. He was bent over fumbling in a desk drawer. "You guys go ahead," he said.

"Oh come on. It'll be fun!" Kenny said.

Ben looked up and sighed. "Okay. I haven't had any fun for a while."

"Yes!" My voice echoed hollow.

In the mirror, I adjusted my silver rimmed glasses. Dad wouldn't get me contact lenses. "You are too young to wear contacts. It might ruin your eyes. It's new technology. Who knows what the side effects might be," he had said. I combed my straight chin length hair, put on a pair of straight jeans and a too-big sweater, perfectly plain Jane, but it was the best I could do. Maria wore glasses too, but she knew the boys and was an inch shorter than Min or I, so she was like their little sister. I didn't know how to behave around boys, having been in girls school since second grade. Gege equally did not know how to talk to me.

The freeway curved. The inside of our car hummed. Sam switched on the cassette tape deck. Carpenters began singing *Yesterday Once More*.

"I love Carpenters!"

There after, they played Carpenters the whole two hour drive to Blackpool Amusement Park.

Maria can cook. Min can smile. I know music. Somehow I had found a place in this group.

Roller coaster

"Wow!" I looked up at the giant roller coaster. We girls had never been to a real amusement park before. Min eyed the cotton candy machine while my eyes were glued to the giant structure, a tingling excitement stirred.

"Wonna go up?" Ben asked Min. Kenny glanced over at me.

"Maybe the small one if Sis would ride with me," Min said.

"Okay I'll go."

Kenny got us tickets. As the small roller coaster turned a sharp corner, Min screamed into my ear as she grabbed me tight, "Sis! I'm going to die!"

I was grinning ear to ear. "You're not going to die."

After we climbed out of our seats. Kenny approached me. "You're not afraid of heights?"

"Must be all the kungfu novels. I've always wanted to jump up and down roof tops. This is pretty close."

"Which ones you like?"

"I like The Heavenly Sword and the Dragon Saber." The book is about searching for two coveted weapons, a heaven-reliant sword and a dragon-slayer saber. Either weapon could rule the martial arts world. It's by Jin Yong or Gum Yoong in the Hong Kong dialect. I've read most of his books.

"But my favorite is The Book and the Sword," I added. It is about a kungfu hero and two princesses of a Muslim country, one beautiful, the other a skilled kungfu fighter. The hero helped them searched for their lost Quran. He later fell in love with both of them. Eventually the beautiful one killed herself to save the hero, so her fighter sister got the man.

"I like that one too," Kenny said.

"You like beauty or ability?"

"Both," Kenny said with a smile. I smiled too, at his round face and round glasses, but my gaze fell on Ben a few steps ahead of us.

Mash everything

For our last dinner at Geges' place, they made soy ginger bone-in-chicken with black mushrooms over steamed rice.

"Better enjoy it. At school, you get mash everything. Mash potatoes, mash peas, mash squash." Ben said.

"You can't tell which is which," Sam said.

"Except by color. Green means peas, yellow squash, white is probably potatoes," Kenny said.

"Or apple sauce," said Sam.

Everyone laughed. I didn't think it was funny. Besides, I was ready to go, knowing the boys house was only a bridge, my real destiny was ahead.

That night I didn't sleep well…

I hugged everyone on my team goodbye. I returned home to an empty dark house at night. At the door, I tried to open it but I discovered I did not have my keys. I found myself left outside of my house in the dark alone…

The school

At the school entrance, Kenny wheeled me my overstuffed luggage and handed me a small plastic bag. "We got you each something." "Take care." His voice softer than usual. Then he turned to help Maria with her suitcase.

My hand waved goodbye. My eyes followed their car until it disappeared around a corner.

"Come on in." I swept aside an unexpected yet familiar ache in my heart, turned to face a tall sandy hair lady holding open the iron gate. Ahead past the gate was a sprawling school compound. In the distance spread a two-story gray stone hundred year old building, its windows dark in the soft afternoon sun.

"Come on in," the lady repeated enunciating more clearly this time.

Maria and I pulled our suitcases through the entrance.

"I'm Mrs. Sampson, your housemistress. Let me show you to your dorm!"

"We are a day early," Maria said.

"That's all right. We have arranged a room for you."

Maria and I looked at each other. Between the two of us, we could figure out what she said.

Mrs. Sampson spoke slowly, "You can stay in the same room tonight. Follow me."

The walnut wood plank floor creaked beneath our feet as we approached the dorm-room, one of many down the dim hallway. In this rectangular room were two long narrow windows, radiator heaters under each window, dark wood chests of drawers, four twin beds and a wash basin near the door. After Mrs. Sampson left us to unpack, I said, "This feels like a haunted mansion."

"Shh, don't say that." Maria pulled out a wooden cross, set it on the dresser top and slammed the drawer shut.

"Good thing you brought that."

"Actually Sam gave it to me."

"Oh, that's what you got. Kenny gave me Book and the Sword book set."

I stomped around to make more noise, to chase away the eerie silence. Our first day at an English boarding school, there were just me, Maria, a housemistress and a few other helpers in this twenty acre school-ground. Maria turned off the light and I sank into the saggy bathtub like mattress...

A creature came into my bed. I screamed, "MARIA!" But no sound came out. I scream repeatedly but still no sound came...

The girls

Next morning, Mrs. Sampson helped us pick out pieces of used school uniform. Our uniform was quite informal. There was no embroidered school emblems, just a grey wool skirt, baby blue light-weight sweater and grey felt blazers. The uniform for Summer term, which spanned from April to June, was even less formal. Any knee length dress with shades from light blue to navy blue would do.

By mid-afternoon, two more students arrived, two German girls, both new students. We formed a pack to explore the school ground. The buildings, most of them a hundred or more years old except two modern ones, the library and the sixth form dorm, formed the perimeter. A driveway cut through two green fields. The larger field was for sports such as field hockey, the smaller one for us to sit or sunbath. The driveway connected the main entrance to a covered walkway which in turn connected the classrooms to the junior dorms where Maria and I stayed. There was also a tennis court and an indoor swimming pool, squash courts and gym. The German girls, Maria and I all spoke little English, but had no problems exploring together.

Around dinner time, the English girls came back. The dorm hallway soon filled with "Hey Ann!" "Hi Trish!" "Jenny!" "Rebecca!" hugs, trunks dragged across wood floor, a few shouts of "bloody hell!" I retreated to my dorm-room to meet my roommates, as did Maria. In my room, I had picked out a firm mattress, my belongings put away, my little corner neat and tidy. My roommates came in one after another.

"Hi there, you new?"

"Yes, I'm Shirley."

"Shirl the pearl! I'm Vicky."

"Heather,"

"Gill,"

"Hi," "Hi," "Hi."

Vicky had a large presence, average height, big dark brown hair, big brown eyes, fair skin, a prominent chin, square shoulder, yet feminine overall. Heather's voice was soft, with soft curly red hair, a fuller body than Vicky. Gill was small with short fine blond hair and a smallish face to match. She checked me out, "What's your Chinese name?"

"Hiu-ha."

"Hu ha?"

"Hiu-ha."

"Huui ha?"

"Just call me Shirley."

"How did Huui Ha become Shirley?"

"From the back of a dictionary."

"You get to pick your own name?"

"Form two teacher from Australia. She made us pick English name."

"So you pick Shirley?"

"It sounds like Snow Lily. I like it."

"Oh, nice."

The girls proceeded to unpack - clothes, books and trinkets all over the floor. I worked on my letter home while they exchanged holiday stories. Soon the mess cleared and walls plastered with posters and family photos. I suddenly became aware my wall was bare.

Maria came in with three Hong Kong girls. My roommates knew them. "Hey Angela Kwok." "Hi Michelle." "Katie Fong!"

The five of us Hongkongers left together to the dinning hall. While waiting at the front of the line outside the yet closed door, chitchat around me was all about a new born baby found in a toilet before the holiday break.

"The baby was dead."

"We think it was Abebi."

"She's not back this term."

I wondered how often that happened.

"Someone gets pregnant every other year."

The eight feet tall double door creaked open and the girls pushed from behind. We all leaned forward and then quickly dispersed through the door. Katie and Michelle rushed in and secured a table for us.

Dinner was boiled fingerling potatoes, boiled peas, cold cut ham and bread pudding with warm custard. Holding forks in my left hand,

I tried to stab the peas. Then I tired to balance them with the knife in my right hand. Half the peas got into my mouth, the other half on my lap. I gave up and reached for the bread pudding.

"Pass the custard please," someone shouted for me.

Michelle Kwok barely touched her plate. She picked up a peach from the center of the table, sliced it down the middle around the pit, then twisted the two half until they broke apart. She sliced each half again into quarters, the pit fell out. She cut quarters into eighths, held the peach slice with two fingers and nibbled the pink flesh, her crisp white linen shirt spotless. I was mesmerized.

After dinner, we visited each others' dorm-rooms. Angela Kwok gave me a magazine and some sticky tack. "Here, you can tear out any pages you like to paste on your wall."

Angela Kwok was Michelle's younger sister. While Michelle had a pretty face, Farrah Fawcett hair, slim except for a wider bottom, Angela was plump all over with straight hair and dark rimmed glasses, but her cashmere full-length dress made her appear rich.

"Michelle and I went shopping at Harrods before coming here," Angela told Katie. The sisters had homes in Nigeria, London and Hong Hong.

Katie Fong came back from Hong Kong. Her signature was Prince Charlies. The wall by her bedside was covered with posters of him. "I'm going to marry him some day," she said. The English girls laughed with her. Katie had short short hair and a big noise. Her thin body was wrapped in an expensive track suit, a pair of latest version Sony Walkman headphone over her ears. We all thought she wasn't serious about Prince Charlies, but could not be sure.

I realized Maria and I had nothing. We were not rich, not pretty, had no "signature." We could be perfectly ignored.

Now that all the girls were back, I had to wait to take a shower in the shared bathroom next door to my room. As I stood with my towel, nightgown and shower caddy in hand, I heard "ergh, argh, urgh!" in a toilet stall. Soon a tall skinny blond girl came out wiping her mouth. I turned toward her. She past me without looking up.

At bedtime, I sat finishing up my letter home. Vicky's boombox played Queen's *Bohemian Rhapsody*. I soon learned Carpenters were not "cool." It had to be something like Queen, The Pretenders, Blondie or Pink Floyd. If one could stomach Van Halen, now that would be something.

"Lights out!" Mrs. Sampson's head poked in just after 10 PM. Gill

14

hopped off her bed and switch off the light. Vicky turned off the boombox. Heather's flashlights came on. I shut my Book and the Sword. A cool fresh English air drifted in from the window by my bed. I snuggled deeper under my duvet and closed my eyes. "Shff shfff creeek," whispered into my drowsy semi-sub-conscious. I squeezed my eyes shut and put the pillow over my face, and fell asleep.

September 12, 1979

Dear Baba, Mama, Didi, Aunt Shan,

How's everyone? I have arrived at school yesterday on September 11. The school actually opens on the 12th, but because Min's school opens on the 11th and for Geges' convenience so they don't have to drive us twice from Birmingham to Bristol, Maria and I arrived here a day early.

Yesterday Gege helped us a lot. They helped Min and I open bank accounts at the National Westminster bank. I deposited £180. Min's account is at a different branch of the same bank. My bank address is National Westminster Bank, 51 Henleaze Road, Westbury-on-Trym, Bristol. Min can tell you her bank address. We each chose a branch closest to our school.

In Birmingham, I spent a total of £18. This includes rent, electricity, food, expenses at Blackpool, gas money, etc. Right now, besides the £180 in the bank, I gave £38 for safekeeping at school. So you don't have to worry I don't have enough money. As for the school uniform, I've already bought some used pieces, but still missing some. I think I can get all used pieces. If not, the school can order new ones. So uniform won't be a problem.

Yesterday when we arrived, Maria and I were the only ones at the whole school. The housemistress, secretary, and schoolmistress are all very kind. They arranged for Maria and I to sleep in the same dorm-room, but tonight we won't be in the same room. They even provided three meals for us, took care of us, often asked if we were comfortable and well. Our housemistress even has a daughter in Hong Kong. She said she can ask her daughter to telephone you to tell you we've arrived safely. This morning, a German student arrived. She is also a new student, so we became friendly quickly. I think this afternoon when the other students get here, it will not be so quiet. Last night was the first night I experienced the lonesome feeling of being away from home without family to care for me. Before that, even though I was away from home, the Geges took good care of us. Now the housemistress and staff help us a lot, but I have to be courteous to them. It feels like there is a barrier between us.

Min has already arrived at Clifton. We went with her and parted ways at her school. I met another girl who went there from Hong Kong. I believe Min will have company, so I'm not too worried about her. I'm sure she'll tell you about her situation herself. I have her phone number, but have to wait until tonight before I can call her. It is very convenient to make phone calls here. I just have to put coins into the phone box, but Min can't make calls as easily, so I will call her often. Anyway even though we can't take care of each other, we can keep in touch easily, so you don't need to worry.

Two more girls just arrived. They are both friendly. There are four of us in this dorm, there is a wash basin in our room, bathroom is next door, very convenient. The school ground is very big and very beautiful. I'll send some photos later.

By the way, we are very happy to know we can come home Christmas. I wonder if we will meet our guardians before we come home. We haven't met them yet. Gege also invited us to stay with them for the four days before we leave for Christmas. We can decide later.

Happiness,

Hiu-ha

September 12, 1979

The school year

On my time-table that first term of form four were nine subjects. I circled EFL (English as a Foreign Language), Math, Physics and Chemistry in the easy group; Biology, History, Geography and French in the difficult group. I put a big red circle around English. Music, Art and Religious Studies were electives. I chose Art. Maria convinced me to take Religious Studies with her. Our class size were about twenty students, half day-schoolers and half boarders.

First week of English class, I could muddle through general reading and even writing, but Shakespeare was impossible.

"To thine own self be true." I could not translate "thou" to "you", "thine" to "your", "doth" to "do" fast enough in my head. The sentences don't even follow the rules I had learned in Hong Kong. "They sparkle still the right Promethean fire," which is the subject and which is the action?

Compared to English EFL was very easy. It was like English class in Hong Kong. There were five of us Hong Kong girls plus two Nigerians. The Nigerian girls were rich like the Kwok sisters. The four of them sometimes from a group and reminisced about Nigeria.

For Physical Education, we had field hockey, which was completely foreign to me. I was more bookworm than athletic, could barely play basketball or swim. After getting whacked on my knees a few times, my teacher switched me to tennis.

In Art class, our project that term was pottery. Miss Elis demonstrated the technique and we set out to make clay pots on our turning wheels.

The girls moulded clay while sang out loud, "We don't need no education. We don't need no thought control."

"Quiet please," Miss Elis said, but was duly ignored.

"Miss Elis, what do you think of this?" Vicky held up a lump of clay in the shape of a very large male anatomy, stroking it up and down. The girls all laughed. Miss Elis left the room. I saw tears down her cheeks.

Once a day, we had self-study periods supervised by prefects. How else could they get us to study, right? Last day of the week, we had our first prefect from Hong Kong.

"Who's that?" I whispered to Angela.

"That's Winnie. She's in form seven. That's how she got to be a prefect."

"Please be quiet," Winnie voice was barely audible.

The girls started singing "We don't need no education."

"Quiet please," Winnie repeated.

This was again ignored. The girls got louder and louder. At that time I needed to go to the bathroom, so I went up to ask for permission. Winnie said, "I can't let you go. If I do, everyone else would want the same and not come back."

I returned to my seat, Vicky and a few other ringleaders eyed me as though I was colluding with Winnie. They quiet down the rest of the period.

First Saturday, we had five hours of free time to go shopping.

"Wear dress or a skirt. Remember no jeans going out," Mrs. Sampson reminded us.

Our school was famous for turning out fine ladies. I soon learned to wear long puffy skirts hiding my jeans underneath. Once outside and out of sight, we shed the skirts.

The nearest shopping area was in Clifton, a short walk from Min's school. Maria and I rode the bus there. We visited Min's dorm and school ground which was much smaller, but it had everything they needed. Min's school was better known for its academics, not a finishing school like mine. Min had made two new friends, both from Hong Kong. The five of us scrolled along cobblestone sidewalks and shopped at quaint little shops that sold candies, pastries, artsy cards and gifts.

"What did you get from Gege?" I asked Min.

"A box of caramel chocolate bonbon."

We window-shopped clothing stores, jewelry, furniture and even sewing material. I soaked in all the colors, shades, textures, sizing proportions - art lessons not taught in class - and envied Min who could come out to this shopping area in jeans and during weekday.

On Sunday, I went with Maria to the chapel. It was in an obscure part of school. We were among the very few there, too quiet and isolated for me. I refused to go with her after that.

Sunday afternoon, the Kwok sisters and Katie showed Maria and I the music building where there were private sound proof rooms for piano practice. Katie taught me to play Chopsticks.

Sunday night after lights out, I closed my eyes to sleep as usual. "Shff shfff creeek." A flashlight shone on my face.

"Hey Shirl," Vicky whispered by my bed, "want to come with us?"

I slipped off my bed and followed them.

In the bathroom, Gill cracked a window, Heather held the flashlight, Vicky shook out cigarettes and lit each one. I gingerly held the smoldering cigarette and put it between my lips but didn't inhale. The girls finished theirs, I threw mine in the toilet. We shuffled back to our room.

The next day, I asked Michelle at lunch, "You smoke?"

"You want to learn?" I said nothing. "We can go after classes."

After classes that day, Maria expected me to go to the library with her. Michelle eyed me, Angela and Katie by her side.

"I'm going with them today," I said.

"We're going to teach Shirley how to smoke. You wanna come?"

Maria walked away. The rest of us followed Katie to the sixth-form dorm. They brought me to Katie's older sister's room, where no-smoking wasn't straightly enforced. The sixth form was still in class. We made ourselves at home. There, I learned to inhale properly and blew circles.

In two weeks, I had learned almost all there was to learn, except sex education. That didn't take long before Vicky tossed me a paperback with a gift wrapped cover. I didn't realized it was very x-rated until part way into the book. After that, I read whatever the girls gave me. I'm sure my general English improved from those books which helped advanced me to the classics.

Once I even witnessed a live show from the grounds keeper and his wife. "Hey look!" Gill said and we all looked up from our books. The pair sat clothed, not far from their window, casually grinding away.

The girls themselves proudly showed off hickeys on their necks after returning from a long weekend.

Maria might be the only one who managed to stay pure. Once in a while, I agreed to go with her to tea with an eighty year old lady living alone. We brought her scones or cucumber sandwiches. She made us tea.

By half-term, which was merely three weeks from start of school, we had our first tests. I received A's and B's in all science classes. In English, I scraped by with a D. French I did surprisingly well, considering I had no foundation.

"How did you do?" Angela asked me.

"B. You?"

"Comme ci comme ça."

She flipped her right hand back and forth to the rhythm of those words. We received the same score which caused some envy and even respect from the Kwok sisters. The sisters had years of tutoring, even spent some time in France in an exchange program. French efficiency, or at least the ability to mix in a few French words in an English sentence, was a requirement in high society.

In my report card that term, teachers commented I "worked well" and was cooperative, but quiet and reserved. In defense, I would say I was busy observing and absorbing, trying to find my place in a strange new world.

Half term

Min and I finally met our guardians for our two week half-term break. Dr. Higgins looked like a typical scholarly doctor, silver glasses, white beard, white hair, average built, average height in a tweed jacket. Mrs. Higgins appeared taller and bigger than Mr. Higgins, brown hair, brown eyes, distinguished nose, chin and jaws, yet soft and feminine in a coral knit top and beige skirt. As far as I know, Dr. Higgins and Dad met in England over some research discussion. Dr. Higgins followed up with visits to my dad in Hong Kong. While Mr. Higgins seemed reserved, Mrs. Higgins was friendly and talkative, except Min and I could understand little of what she said.

"How's your father?"

"He's fine. Thank you Mrs. Higgins."

"You can call us Margo and Hugh."

Margo said something about busy moving to a new "cottage" in the countryside and hadn't found time to see us sooner. Once she discovered we could not really carry on a conversation, the hour long car ride turned quiet, and I enjoyed my first scenic tour of the British countryside.

While the outskirts of Bristol were run down with housing projects and graffiti, further north were rolling green hills, scattered light brown stone huts and occasional spread of sheep and cattle pastures.

Our car slowed down at Cirencester, I was elated to see a quint little town adorned with a spired cathedral, restaurants and shops, but the car kept going. When we finally stopped, it was already dark. My mood dimmed. We had arrived at a farm house. It was so dark I could not make out my surrounding.

Inside was a low ceiling "cottage." Hugh placed logs in a fireplace built within a low beige brick wall. Books filled a built-in bookshelf set in the same brick wall. We dined pork chop, buttered mushrooms and potatoes which Margo had prepared ahead of time. After dinner, Margo showed us our rooms upstairs. Mine was a small dome like attic turned bedroom, wallpapered with narrow blue and white stripes, decked with soft beddings of Laura Ashley pattern…

Water leaking and pouring down my face. I woke up and went to the sink to get a pot to hold the gushing water leak. The leak was coming out of a broken pipe on the wall, not from rain seeping through the ceiling…

I woke in a soft dry bed. Down stairs in bright sunlight, I discovered a large backyard.

"The garden is a bit wild now," Margo said.

"It's beautiful," said Min.

After a breakfast of sausage, toast and soft boiled egg, Hugh took us out for a walk. This cottage was in the famed Cotswolds area where buildings were typically two stories dressed in beige-gold-colored stones skirted with trimmed hedges. Sheep pastures, climbing vines, wood fences, wild blue and raspberry bushes spread farther out. Hugh explained the vegetation in the area as a typical scientist. Min and I collected small bluebells, buttercups and daisies.

"Pretty flowers. We should make cards for you to send home," Margo said when we returned. We placed the flowers inside a heavy book.

"When they dry, we arrange them on paper cards and seal them with clear plastic press." She showed us some samples so we could understand.

Afternoon tea was jam rolls, sardine or liver pâté on toast, black tea served with cream and little cubes of sugar. We sipped, nibbled and chatted. They showed us photos of their son and daughter, both away attending universities. Chris was studying agriculture, Jenny medicine.

"Jenny is a very good student," Hugh said. "I wish Chris would try harder."

"Jenny's too hard on herself sometimes," said Margo, "I'm afraid she's getting bulimic."

I couldn't tell if they were speaking to us or each other, so kept quiet. By then I had learned bulimia was caused by vomiting out food after meals. A girl would put her finger deep into her throat which causes a gag reaction and vomit. A cheat to stay slim.

On the weekend, Margo took us shopping in Cirencester. We went to Woolworth department store. Margo shopped for mincemeat pie which was made with dried fruit, not meat.

The four of us visited the cathedral.

"Everything here is so old," I commented.

"It's history," Hugh said.

Min made a face.

"You don't like history?"

"We prefer modern things," I answered for Min.

"Someday when you're our age, you'll appreciate antiques."

When neighbors greeted us, Margo and Hugh would call us their Chinese daughters. They were nothing like our mom and dad who were overly concerned about our school work, achievements and future. Margo and Hugh educated and nurtured without expectations.

Within two weeks, Min and I could carry on simple conversations with them, as long as it was not jokes or politics, and I started to catch bits and pieces. "Strikes." "Picketing." "No one bury the dead." "Rats and rubbish all over." "IRA bombing." "Prime minister Margaret Thatcher."

Still, time went too slowly. "There's nothing to do," Min and I whispered to each other. When half-term break ended, we were happy to return to the city, and our friends at school.

Christmas

That year, the school closed four days before we leave for Hong Kong for Christmas. I asked if Min and I could stay at Geges' place for the four days. Dr. Higgins was in Trinidad for a long work trip. Mrs. Higgins went with him. Their travel schedules were often sporadic.

"We want you to visit Mr. and Mrs. Cayton. They offered to host you. Give them a call." Mom was always concerned about us young girls with boys. When she initially found out Maria and we were going to England together, she was relieved. She didn't know we were staying with boys.

Mr. and Mrs. Cayton were Irish, in their sixties, both short and plump, with rosy cheeks. Their house was packed full of bits and pieces of antique furniture, paintings, cups, vases and other odds and ends. Mrs. Cayton loved to cook, so Min and I spent most of our time in their kitchen helping and then in the dinning room eating. We understood little of Mr. Cayton, with his Irish accent, and even less of Mrs. Cayton. This meant I did not enjoy staying at their place. They had a divorced daughter we call Miss Priest who was in Hong Kong. Min and I became occasional messenger and courier between Miss Priest and the Caytons.

Trips

Min and I had become competent travelers. For the journey back to school, we would take the express train from Heathrow airport to Paddington train station and from there to Bristol with a change over at Redding. The only help we sometimes needed was an English gentleman to carry our heavy luggage up or down stairs.

In the Summer term of 1980, the school organized a field trip to Paris. Maria and I joined. The Kwok sisters did not. "We've been there many times," Angela said. Katie declined as well, with the same reason.

We took the train to Dover. We girls decked out in long skirts, strappy flats, shoulder bags, colorful scarfs, loose sweaters - a whirl of blue, some grey, a little white and splashes of pink and purple. Our train cart filled with giggles, murmurs and exclamations. "We don't need no education…" "Hey look!" Finger pointing. "Dishy!" Giggles. Spilled soda pop. "Bloody hell!" "Watch your manners, girls." "What'd you think?" Head down. "Let'm see." Shoulder leaned over.

I took a window seat. Maria by my side. She brought snacks. I looked out the window. It was one of my secret hobbies to zone out in a car or train, zone in the scenery. Maria turned around to talk to other girls.

"Hey look!" I perked up to see the white cliffs of Dover.

When we arrived at Paris. I wasn't impressed. "This is it?" I'm sure it was because we didn't get to sit at a sidewalk cafe and sip coffee.

First, Louvre Museum - Lots of walking. David statue - "Bloody hell!" We studied it, "not David?" Mona Lisa - "Can't see. It's so small." Pompidou - "Wicked!" We ran around, up and down.

Later in the year, Maria, some new friends and I made our own trip to Bath. It was my first sight of a densely packed historic city. More cobblestones. Lots and lots of old buildings and cathedrals. River. Stone arch bridges. Pretty gift shops. People. I loved it even though it was old.

February 21, 1981

Dear Baba, Mama, Didi, Aunt Shan,

How are you? I'm at half-term break. Min's at Mrs. Higgins' place. I'm staying at the form six dorm. It's nice here. There is a full kitchen in this building. Currently I'm staying in a single room. I have my own desk in the room so convenient for homework. Next year when I get to form six, I'll be staying here.

We have made a lot of food! This morning we cooked porridge. It's not as good as at home (because we don't have enough ingredients). But because we haven't eaten porridge for a long time, it tasted extra delicious. This afternoon we plan to make beef rice. I'm salivating even thinking about it. You must be stuffed with New Year Cakes at home! Are you done with New Years holiday yet? Didi got many red packets? Thinking about it, I wonder when we will have a chance to spend Chinese New Year at home.

Mama asked about university tuition. Currently Science curriculum yearly is £3000 to £4000. This is only tuition. Logging extra. Min's school has a student from Hong Kong who could not go to university because of the tuition increase. I feel sorry for her. Hopefully tuition will come back down in two years. In this next two years, they need to get rid of a lot of foreign students. I heard Australia is more open to foreign students. Maybe Didi can try to go to Australia. For me, I can go anywhere. As long as I can go to a university.

As for what subjects to take, I have probably already mentioned in my last letter. I plan on taking Physics, Chemistry and Math. I have asked my teachers, they all said I should have no problems. As for what I want to do in the future, I don't know yet. Our school has a Hong Kong student taking A Level exam this year. She got three A's in the mock exam. It is very difficult to get A's in A Level, not to mention three A's. She wants to study Civil Engineering. Is this a good career? But I think this is a difficult career for women. And I need to be as smart as this girl. She told us teachers are important, but a big part depends on ourselves. Of course we need natural talent. She has both. There are already four universities offering her with low requirements. She said our Physics teachers not too good. The others are so so. Also our form has a student applying to Haileybery boarding school. This English girl went to the interview. She said there are 150 applicants. Only 60 made it to the interview level. And they only accept 20. No wonder I got rejected right away.

Have you received my report card? My form teacher let me look at the comments. She said I have a very good report card this year. But I look and look and can't tell the difference between this one and the previous ones. I think they are about the same.

Happy to hear Mama's coming early. I hope you can come look at my school, talk to my teachers and check out our dorms. When Baba comes, our holiday won't start yet. If Baba goes to Bath first, you can come see us! Also for Easter can we stay at Baba's residence hall? If we can we don't have go to Miss Priest's or Caytons'.

Have to stop now. Hope to see you seen! Didi make sure you study hard. Don't complain I nag, but it's important you build a good foundation.

Wish happiness and health!

Respectfully,

Hiu-ha

February 21, 1981

P. S. Enclosed photos are taken with Higgins' son and daughter.

March 16, 1981

Dear Baba, Mama, Didi, Aunt Shan,

How are you? When my letter reaches you, Dad is already on his way here. Are you busy packing? Don' know where your first stop would be, London or Bath? Call us when you get here, okay? My school number is 611247 Bristol. Can't believe I'll see you all so soon! Didi you stay home alone can watch TV all day long? Aunt Shan, you have to keep an eye on him!

Yesterday Miss Priest invited us to her house for dinner. She told us a lot about Hong Kong, and about you taking her to the airport, give her presents, etc. She's been back for a month, has been busy through Easter. She has not asked us to stay with her, even though I have hinted. She said if Mama comes, go there for dinner. Since she has no intention of hosting us, we haven't said anymore. Two more weeks and it's Easter. We don't know where we will stay. Mrs. Cayton said she will write or telephone, but still no news. I'll call them this evening, don't worry. We'll think of something. If go to Caytons, their phone number is Bristol 624006. The other possibility is stay with a friend. (The one who gave us Laopo Cake.) That phone number is 01-567-1605 (no need to dial the code number). If Mama can't understand the telephone system here, ask your friend who is coming with you at Easter. It is coming up so soon, I am not prepared.

My EFL exam result has come out. I got an A. This is the same as the one Min took last summer. It was easy.

I just called Mrs. Cayton. Finally decided to go to Mrs. Higgins first week March 3 to April 1, because Cayton not available. April 1 we come back to Bristol to go the Caytons'. Min said you have her school phone number. Baba when you come you can call her school to find her.

Finally found out our summer holiday dates. My exam finish on June 19. I can leave on the 19th. School starts September 7. Even though we have the same exam dates, Min's school won't let them leave early, but I can leave early. Can you book a separate flight for Min?

By the way I have no problems with school grades this term. I think I can rank second in class. Physics I already got used to our teacher's style. He is actually very good, can open our mind, not like the others who teach by stuffing our brains full.

Wish Mama's work go smoothly, quickly finish so you come happily.

As for you Didi, you are lucky to have a new Hi-Fi. I remember when we were home, Baba got mad with me every time I turned up pop music. Can't believe Didi can now listen to pop. You have to be a good boy and study hard at home when Mama and Baba are here!

Respectfully,

Hiu-ha

March 16, 1981

Form five

Our school year had three terms. Spring term was January to April. Summer April to June. Autumn September to December. Our O Level exam was in June of 1981. That year, everyone's main concern became school work, even Vicky and her group of girls settled down. We abandoned all the electives. I had made cups, bowls, knitted a sweater and even sawn a skirt from Art class, but remembered nothing from Religious Studies.

To relief stress, our freetime was spent watching an American evening soap opera called Dallas. Everyone crowded in front of the TV in the common room and marveled at the tight fitting dresses, big hairdo of Sue Ellen and sexy long hair flawless face of Pamala. The English girls rolled their tongues to speak like Texans.

One frequent "news" among the girls was "end of the world." "Thursday is the end of the world," someone would say and others would concur, "it's in the news." Pressure under the looming exam was so high that "end of the world" was not considered bad news. But the day would come and gone. I soon learned to ignored them.

An English girl told us another news, "My brother's friend got stabbed to death on holiday." Her brother and friend went to Southern France for holiday.

"What! Who killed him?"

"Some Nazi. They had an argument..."

It was then that I understood the subtle tension between the English and German girls, an animosity carried over from World War II. The rich Hong Kong girls were in a relatively higher social hierarchy.

That year, the Irish Republican Army intensified their terroristic bombing; it was the Irish Catholics verses the English Protestants, or the subjugate verses its ruler; I'm not sure which. The Kwok sisters reduced their visits to Harrods the luxury department store, which was a main target of the IRA, especially during holiday shopping. Even our flight that summer from London to Hong Kong was diverted to Bahrain overnight because of a bomb scare, so Min and I had a free day trip to the Arabia continent. From our bus to the hotel, we gawked at shops upon shops along desert streets selling gold blocks.

The strikes also intensified, spreading from hospitals and sanitation workers to steel miners. Trains and buses stopped a few times. British economy started a downward slide. University tuition increased sharply.

In Geography class, one English girl asked, "Are we still the most powerful country in the world?" I snickered under my breath.

One cold day when filling the bathtub at Hugh and Margo's cottage, Hugh reminded us to fill no more than an inch of water. I compared the situation in England against the glamor in the Dallas TV show. That was the last push needed for me to apply for American colleges. Mom and Dad liked the idea because tuition would be cheaper. The only reason we could afford to go to England was my dad's position as a professor. The Hong Kong University paid for our tuition and plane tickets. Grandpa Cuan paid all the other expenses. Dad made sure I did not forget. "We are not wealthy enough to send you all overseas. You need to watch your expenses."

Min and Maria decided to stay in England.

My letters home had become all about school grades, university applications and where to stay for holidays. Each year, the boarding school closed for four long weekends and three half-term breaks. This means at least seven times a year we had to figure out a place to go. The pressure then was on me to find lodging for Min and I. I hated this, but somehow or another we always had a roof over our heads, thanks to Maria, and my ability to make new friends. The Kwok sisters never invited me to their London home. Financial declaration was another frequent topic to write home, for every university required proof of funds as part of their application process.

May 15, 1981

Dear Baba, Mama, Didi, Aunt Shan,

Sorry I haven't written last week, because there is nothing special to write. Besides Min already told you everything, so I didn't write. Two more weeks and it will be the exam. The atmosphere at school is getting tense. Because I didn't study well for the last mock exam, I'm now facing a desk full of books, a bit lost as to how to handle it all. But I'm better than most English girls. I've studied harder. Mama you don't need to worry about me not getting enough sleep, etc. I'll never pull late nights. Besides there is no chance. This place is very strict. Lights out every night at 10 PM sharp, after that we can't use even a flash light. Also whenever I have free time, I go play tennis to relax.

Next Thursday is open house. This time I haven't had to help. Probably because I didn't do a good job last time. Teachers didn't want my help anymore :) Actually us form five don't have much to do, probably they know we are busy.

I heard Hong Kong is extremely hot, even has water restriction, is this true? It is cold here. Have to wear a light coat. When the sun comes out, it gets warm. We can already wear summer uniform, but have to wear a coat outside to stay warm. So now it is short sleeve inner layer, light coat outer layer, looks weird. Also have you heard from the news that some Ireland prisoners went on hunger strike? Two people already died. There's unrest here. In Ireland there are riots.

Baba have you got us entry card for the sports center? We really want to play tennis or swim. Still a month until we come home, but already thinking what we want to do when we get home. This time we have two months holiday! Also have you sent the plane tickets? Because we haven't received them yet.

Didi you lazy bug, have you worked hard on homework? I've told you hundreds of time to send us letters but you haven't. You'll get a taste of my wrath when we get home. Mama also, haven't written a letter. This term I only got one letter. Next time I write, exam will have started. I'll write if I have time then!

Hiu-ha, respectively.

May 15, 1981

September 9, 1981

Dear Grandpa Cuan, Grandma Cuan, Uncle Manuel, Cousin David,

How are you? Few days ago when you called and we didn't get to talk to you, we feel sorry. We had really wanted to hear your voice, but unfortunately it was too late. We were all sleeping. Mama didn't wake us up. But Mama said you had a great time in the US. We are happy for you.

This holiday Min and I both had a taste of summer job. Min tutored two kids, earned $500. I went to work at Lane Crowfort department store for three weeks as a sales clerk. This job is not easy. Nine to six everyday. We have to work even on Sundays. Even though it was hard work, I learned a lot of things I can't learn from school. I feel it had been very meaningful. Plus I made $900. Besides work, Min and I also busy studied, preparing for the US TOFEL and SAT. Now I have already applied to some universities. I'll see if any school will accept me. Tuition in England is just too expensive.

During summer Cousin Yee, Aunt Kay and Cousin Greg had all come to visit Hong Kong. Aunt Kay and Cousin Greg stayed at our home three weeks. When they first got here, because Cousin can't understand Chinese, we had to speak to him in English. At first it was hard to get used to it, but we quickly became friends.

Mid Autumn Festival is almost here. I wonder if you have plans to celebrate? I am lucky to be home this year to celebrate the festival. It is because school doesn't open until September 16. Sadly for Min, her school started early. She is already back in England. I guess you must have taken many photos in the US. Can you send us some? We really want to see if Grandpa and Grandma have gain some weight, if Cousin David have gotten taller, if he can measure up to Didi. I won't write anymore. Grandpa, Grandma and Uncle you take care of your health. I should ask Grandma again, you need to eat more! I'll write again when I get back to England.

We wish you health and happiness!
Respectfully,
Hiu-ha, Hiu-min, Hiu-fai
September 9, 1981

Summer job

Lane Crowfort summer job was my first time in a co-ed environment since second grade in China. There were about twenty students. I noticed one boy right away who was tall and slim, who looked like the main actor who was cast as Chan in the TV version of the Book and the Sword. He worked in the next department over. I was in Men's Suit. He was in Men's Ties. Lane Crowfort was a huge high end department store, my family didn't shop there. Men's Ties and Men's Suite departments were large enough that I could only see "Chan" if I moved all the way to the left side of my counter and lean my body way over, and if he happened to stay still. Even then I was too self-conscious to actually peek at him.

My job was to stand behind at a counter to greet customers and direct questions to my manager. Eventually I graduated to take orders and even helped with measurements.

Didi and Mom came to visit me two weeks after I started work. Didi, my brother Fai was thirteen years old, but looked to be at least seventeen, with deep set eyes, thick brows, six foot two inches tall, shoulders wide enough to protect two of me. Mom was not short herself at five foot five inches. She wore an elegant A-line dress of small-print flowers, her hair set in loose curls colored ebony black.

"I didn't expect your mom to look like that. She looks young and sophisticated," my manager said.

"Is that your young brother? I thought he was your boyfriend," my counter partner Lily said.

They passed through Men's Ties department on the way out. My heart fluttered when I saw Didi talk to "Chan." He would for sure notice me now. But that was the only conversation we had, indirectly through Didi for a few seconds. Chan and I never even said "Hi" to each other, but I kept him in my heart.

Back at school when Michelle studied the group photo of my summer job interns, she said, "He's just okay. You're still the prettiest in the group."

That was my only "romantic" encounter before entering university, unless if I count Angela Kwok's "love" letter to me. She wrote something like, "I like you a lot." "Want to be best friends." And maybe more, but no sexual innuendo. I read it with the tingling sensation of having an admirer, but the feeling disappeared quickly. I threw away the letter and and pretended I never read it.

November 3, 1981

Dear Baba, Mama, Didi, Aunt Shan,

Just finished half-term now back at school. I gave the Higgins their gift. They both loved it.

Today I received Mama's letter. I'll ask school for the receipt. Enclosed is an application form from Texas Austin. The sixth row is the Financial Declaration. Also University of Wisconsin-Madison and University of Washington-Seattle both need bank letters, but no forms to fill. Texas Austin deadline is Feb 1. Washington is May 1. Even though some university deadline is later, but a letter sent from you to Grandpa Cuan then from grandpa back to me then for me to send to university takes much time, so better to send to grandpa early. Hope you don't feel all these is much hassle. This is all the universities I have applied. I have not time to apply to the new university recommended by Baba's colleague. I can just apply these three first.

I have a lot of homework now, but can still catch up. Also for math test I received the highest mark in class, 54/60. Math is easy so far. I still have much to study for Physics and Chemistry. Tests are coming up.

This Christmas I am invited to stay at a friends house, the one I met at Lane Crowfort. She and I got to know each other pretty well. Min have also met her. She is very nice and honest. So you don't need to worry. The house belongs to her (Lily) classmate Jenny's uncle. The whole house will have Lily, Jenny and her uncle and aunt, all together five of us. This way you only have to pay for Min's ticket home.

Baba's work trip to Singapore fun? Didi have you kept up studying hard, or have you slacked off again? Remember you said you won't disappoint me this time, will get A honor? Hope you don't eat your words. Actually if you would just listen to Aunt Shan, do your

40

homework right after school and review a little textbook, you will have no problems with good grades.

Ok, have to stop here.

Wish all well,

Hiu-ha

November 3, 1981

P. S. Have you received my report card and O Level result?

Form six

When I eventually received my O Level result, my English grade was an E, a fail grade. But they let me retake.

"Your writing is inconsistent. You don't need to use big words. Your best stories are told using simple words you are comfortable with. Your essay can pull up your grade," Mrs. Wilson, my English teacher, told me.

I remembered her words and passed the retake with a B!

Form six, we moved into the modern building. No more creaky floors and dark wood furniture! For freetime, Angela, Katie and I congregated in Michelle's single occupancy room. We slurped cup noodles, browsed fashion magazines, smoked, listened to the latest pop songs, reminisced about Hong Kong, watched Michelle paint her nails or style her hair.

My hair had grown long, my complexion lighter after two years of little-sun-much-mist English weather. My dad finally let me wear contact lenses.

During the last form six half-term break, I permed my hair for the first time. It was a medium tight curl in shoulder length. The waves covered my forehead making my eyes appeared recessed and deep, while the curls on the side made my face more chiseled which was the "in" look.

When I returned to school, Michelle said, "Wow, you look like Emma!"

Emma was a fair face, dark brown curly hair day-school girl everyone considered beautiful. But also big hair was becoming the fashion. My long hair once permed became the biggest hair of them all.

For our form six sherry party, I put on a loose straight cut black jersey dress paired with black ballerina flats. Two years of soaking in fashion magazine and Kwok sisters' company had rubbed off on me. I knew to shop for cheap clothes in high fashion style.

"What a beautiful dress. Where did you get that?"

When I didn't reply, Michelle stepped behind me and flipped over my back collar.

"Oh," she said cooly. It was a no name brand.

Katie's appearance had also dramatically changed after half-term. She still had short short hair, but her face was glowing translucent, her eyes turned "double-lidded." She wore a white shirt, striped burgundy skirt, white stockings and low heels. Prince Charlies and Diana's wedding didn't dampen her spirit, not even a little bit, but she took down all her posters of the prince.

Angela got contact lenses too, and a new silky straight bob cut parted off side, but she still looked about the same, as did Michelle and Maria.

All the teachers and our new headmaster attended the sherry party, held by the school for us sixth and seventh form boarding students. There were about ten Hong Kong girls, thirty some English girls, a handful of German and other Europeans, two girls from Nigeria, a few from Southeast Asia and India. By then I had become closer friends with Yit, a Malaysian Chinese whose first language was English and spoke no Chinese. We both liked to read, liked to avoid drama and spotlight, not religious good girls, not from wealthy families. Unlike me, she commanded a bigger presence with a larger frame and louder voice.

At these sherry parties, we learned to pair white wine with brie or camembert cheese, held wine glasses with two fingers and made charming little remarks about books, art or culture.

Hugh and Margo commented I had turned into a charming lady. This charming lady decided to quit A Level and head to the United States. Halfway through Spring term in form six, the University of Wisconsin in Madison sent me an offer letter, and I decided to go.

"You are talented in Math. You can go to Oxford or Cambridge, why a no name school?" Mrs. Norris, my math teacher, protested. Our headmaster worded more strongly in my report card, "I think Shirley has made a mistake in considering American universities."

I couldn't wait to go to my American university, even requested to start that summer, which Wisconsin approved. My friends were happy for me. Yit gave me a horny frog parting gift. We all had a good laugh. "At least you know where you'll be going." They still had to face the dreaded A Level exam while I slacked off the rest of the school term. My teachers stopped saying I "worked well" or "worked hard." Instead they said I seemed "unsettled..."

Next I know, I was in Mr. Lee's living room, in a dark corner by myself. Mr. and Mrs. Lee came in through the patio door with their great white sheep dog. I said something to them and Mrs. Lee was saddened.

"But this is your home. Where would you go?" She said.

Tears welled up in my eyes. Holding them back, I said, "I'm going to find my own home."

Then I turned to the main door of the living room, pulled it open and faced a wide open space in hazy white light. I let my tears flow. Where would I go? ...

2

First day in Wisconsin

The flight attended bent over toward me, "What would you like to drink?" I was in a window seat of a British Airway A300.

"A glass of Chardonnay please," my voice loud and clear.

She brought me the Chardonnay in a rounded tumbler. "Can I take a look at your ID?"

I fished out my passport and handed it to her. She studied it. "Sorry you have to be twenty one to drink."

"Oh?!" I handed the tumbler back to her, careful not to spill on my neighbor. So much for thinking I had graduated to be an adult, at least the British thought so. I could travel alone, I was wearing a cashmere vest, my hair was curled, I could speak English clearly and even charmingly. But at that moment I was quickly brought back down a few levels.

It was evening when I exited the jetway at the Madison regional airport. I had been to airports at Bombay, Rome, Bahrain, not to mention London and Hong Kong, but this one was different. There were no crowds of people.

"Excuse me. Where is the main terminal?" I asked an attendant, an older gentlemen with a rounder middle than a typical Englishman.

"Main terminal?" He looked puzzled. "This is the only terminal."

"Oh. Where is the concierge? I'm supposed to get picked up by a university shuttle."

"There's no concierge here. And I haven't heard of university shuttles. You can take a taxi. It's cheap to go to the U. What's the name of your hotel?"

"Er, I don't know. I thought the U had booked one for me."

My calm and confident demeanor must have changed, because the gentlemen smiled kindly and said, "If you like, I can help you book a hotel."

We found a cheap room closest to the university.

June 11, 1982

Dear Baba, Mama, Didi, Aunt Shan,

I have already arrived at Madison last night. The trip was smooth. In New York there was an International Student Service person who came to meet me at the gate. He helped a lot, helped me find the shuttle to La Guardia for the connection. I arrived two hours early. Also no one booked any hotel for me. I called when I was in London, there was no answer. I called again in New York, also no answer. At Madison, the airport person said there is no such service as booking hotels for students. Luckily they offered to help me call around for hotels and helped me booked a room. This room is $26 per night. Meals not included. But it is the cheapest one they could find. This morning I went to the school and they arranged a host family where I can stay for a few days. In a little while I'll give back this hotel room and go there. Also I went to the U's Housing Office and found a place to stay, moving on Sunday. But this dorm I can only stay until the end of Summer term. After Summer I haven't a place to stay yet. U dorms for Fall are already all full, but I will use this time to find a different place. Registration is not until Monday. Summer housing rent is $520 per term including meals. Also the school wants us to buy Health Insurance. It will be about $20 per month. I haven't found a bank to exchange money yet. But rent is not due right now, so I think I have enough money to last one to two weeks.

Madison here is beautiful. There is a lake nearby. Like Cambridge the whole city mostly belongs to the U. The rest is residential. I haven't been to town yet. For what I know there are very few shops. Weather here is very warm. Can wear short sleeves, but not hot.

My dorm address is:

213 SHOWERMAN-KRONSHAGE,

MADISON, WI 53706
U.S.A
Enclosed is a form Dad has to fill out.
Won't write much more. I'm very well. Write again later.
Wish all well!
Respectfully,
Hiu-ha
June 11, 1982

Host family

The host family's house felt like a messy sixth form dormitory. It was spacious, but cluttered at the same time. The kitchen island and counter were covered with plates, pots, cooking appliances, paper napkins, cereal boxes. Everyone wore t-shirts and shorts. The adults did not bother to hide the rolls bulging under their shirts. My first meal was at a picnic table on their deck. The mother laid potato chips and noodle salad on my paper plate.

"Try this. I bet they don't have it in England." She scooped a green and white layered soft cake like substance onto my plate. "It's marshmallow jelly."

"Here is your brat," the father handed me a long bun wrapped around a longer version of the English sausage, dripping with Ketchup. "Bet they don't have this in England either."

I held the brat with both hands and took a bite, ketchup oozed out onto my paper plate, some ended up on my blouse. Everyone ate chips with their fingers, forks in their right hand. Mrs. fired questions at me. "Which part of England?" "Your parents not worried?" "Why Wisconsin?"

"Mom can I go now?" Their seventeen year old girl said. Soon the girl and their older boy disappeared.

"You want to play on my computer?" The twelve year old asked me.

'Good idea, Luke. Show her the basement." "Molly you can go too."

Luke led me downstairs. Molly followed behind. Three computers lined up on a narrow bench table against one wall. Tape decks, electronics and wires scattered about. I had had some Basic programming lessons during form-six, when our whole class shared one computer, now three in one family.

"Can you play Pac Man?"

"No. What's that?"

"I can teach you. It's really easy."

Soon I was squealing, my fingers banging hard on the keys. "Ooohhhh no!" "Aah!"

"You've got it." "Go left." "Get the fruit!" "Yes!"

That night, I slept restlessly...

I was sitting on a bench seat at a rectangular table alone waiting for my friend. One end of this table was butted against a wall covered with a pastel flowery wallpaper. I was at the aisle side of the bench seat with room enough for another person to my left. The flowery wall was to my left. Two guys came to sit across from me. They said something which made me turn to the wall. I saw my friend sitting there, with her left shoulder touching the wall and leaning far from me, such that a big space was between us. "Hey I didn't know you're here already. How long have you been here?" I said to my friend. Then I noticed she was wearing a flowered shirt of a similar color and pattern as the wallpaper, so that she blended into the wall. I almost could not see her...

The next day, father and older daughter asked if I wanted to go play tennis. I might have told them I played.

"I'll just watch," I said.

The three of us approached the fenced-in tennis court. As they went in, I heard the father said to the daughter, "Why does she just want to watch?"

It was the first time I ever heard someone talked behind me. Somehow it hurt. He must have hit me where it hurt. As I sat outside the chain-link fence watching them play, I thought, "They're not that good. I could have played." But I sat. And waited for the next day so I could move into the dorm.

Lakeshore dorm

Kronshage hall was one of many student residences along the south side of Lake Mendota. A pedestrian pathway separated the lake from the dormitories. My room was large with an old wood desk and a bunkbed, but I had the room all to myself. Sitting at the desk, I could see a stretch of green shrubbery along the shore, and beyond that the water. Showerman-Kronshage that summer was co-ed, but still only half full. The place was again too quiet for me. No one ran up and down the hallway shouting "bloody hell." The American men in the dorm to me were like aliens. They did not see me, and I did not see them. I started to miss the English girls.

But the Wisconsin sun was bright and warm. Most days I took my letter writing materials out to the slopped lush green lawn facing the lake - to catch glimpses of sail boats, wind surfers or crew boats cut up the water. One such day a man with freckles and red hair stopped in front of me.

"Nice day isn't it?" "You new here?"

I answer him politely.

"You want to go have a drink?" He said at some point.

"No thank you," I smiled. The man looked older than a typical student. I had been instructed to avoid "aliens," especially old ones. Still, it was the first time anyone had ever asked me out. I had to tell Michelle. I wrote a letter to the Kwok sisters and Katie about my encounter. They did not reply.

Meanwhile social events started popping up among summer students. During one of the multi-dorm barbecue picnic, I met Malia. At first I couldn't tell her nationality. She had thick eye brows, dark skin and a boyish figure.

"Ni xin lai de ma?" Turned out she was the only Chinese around, but she came from Singapore and spoke only English and Mandarin. I spoke Hong Kong Chinese, not Mandarin Chinese, and so we ended up speaking English to each other.

"All these people here seem to be older than you or I," was my first comment to Malia.

"Most regular students leave for the summer. Many of these here are senior or grad students, even outsiders." Malia herself was a junior. Through her, my immediate group became Malia, Sally and Yoko. Yoko was almost three inches taller than me, slim, stylish and beautiful enough to be a model. I had thought Japanese were all short and bow legged. Sally to me was like Sally Field in Smoky And The Bandit, but with short hair and thick glasses. She invited us to her home in Milwaukee, and to my very first baseball game between the Brewers and the Red Sox. I soaked in the crowd and the atmosphere, but the home-runs happened only when I looked away.

On Fridays Malia and I would invade the apartment of a Hong Kong girl, another one of Malia's friends, who had her own apartment. There we cooked and ate Chinese food.

And so the summer breezed by quickly.

August 8, 1982

Dear Baba, Mama, Didi, Aunt Shan,

I've finished my exams. Now we have two weeks before Autumn semester starts. I'm now living at a friend's house. She went to Canada for holiday, so her apartment is empty. She's the one I told you about before. The one we go to cook and eat every Friday. Me and another friend are now living there. This place has two bedrooms, a living room and kitchen. We can cook Chinese food. The one I'm sharing with is from Singapore. She is very nice.

Next semester I'll be living in the dorm, but because I applied late, have to live in the kitchen. They converted kitchens on every floor into dorm-rooms for three people to share. When someone move out of the regular dorm, we can move in. I heard it takes a week or at most a month. I don't know which kitchen I'll be staying at right now, so I don't have an address for you. As for this apartment, I'll be here for only two weeks. Your letters won't reach me for now, but you can send to the lakeshore dorm. The U will forward to my new dorm. Once I have the new address, I'll let you know right away.

My exam results are pretty good. I got A's in both Math and Psychology. School should send you my grades.

Grandpa and Grandma Cuan told me they are well. Still have not moved to California yet.

I've received the three letters Mama sent. It seems each time I sent one out, I receive yours. What type is Mama's bladder infection? Hope not serious. Are you recovered? You have to rest more! Baba has already told you not to get stressed out. You need to spend more time at home, plant some flowers, or watch TV. How's Baba? How was the conference in England? Has Didi received any news from the boarding schools? Do you know which one you are going? I thought Min would write to me soon, but when I moved out of the dorm yesterday, I still haven't received any word. Lost yourself having too much fun? Is Aunt Shan's hand well again? You have to take care of yourself!

This summer I have spent a little more than US$1800. Tuition was originally $790, but because I added psychology, it became $893. Rent was $520, books about $60. Next semester rent reservation is $150. Plus health insurance is $40. Also spent about $100 for daily expenses such as alarm clock, hair dryer, stationary and so on. After all is added up, I wonder if it is still cheaper than UK?

As for boyfriend, I know what to do. I believe I have ability to judge people. Mama you really don't need to worry. When I have a boyfriend I will let you know. The American family I told you about has a middle age couple and four children. The oldest girl is seventeen. Second son is fifteen. Plus another son and daughter about twelve and ten. It's been a month since I saw them. I've been busy so have they. All for now. Everyone take care.

Wish all health!

Respectfully,

Hiu-ha,

August 8, 1982

Ken

Now Malia had an older cousin Ken. I had met him once or twice during the summer. He was a junior like Malia, but two years older. This was because Ken was from Singapore where all men must go through military training for two years before they could enter universities. Ken was built like a sumo wrestler - big, round, with a pudgy face and square glasses. He felt familiar to me, like a big brother.

"So what are you studying?" Ken said.

"Some kind of Engineering. Probably Chemical Engineering."

Ken raised an eye brow, "You're going into Engineering? It's very competitive here you know. Many top of the class high schoolers drop out."

"Calculus is pretty easy so far."

"It will get much harder. Malia gets straight A's. She can help you." Malia was majoring in Computer Science.

"Thanks, but I'm doing okay right now." I was top of the class out of twenty, still, Ken's words made me doubt myself, but then I learned Ken was not good at Math. He didn't need to. He just needed a Bachelors Degree to go into his father's business.

When the results came out at the end of summer, I immediately flaunted my 4.0 GPA to Ken.

"Well, looks like we have another four pointer in our group." Turning to Malia, he said, "Did you ask Shirley if she wants to go?"

"Not yet." "Shirley, Ken and two other Singaporeans are doing a road trip out east. You wanna go?" "If you go, then I can go. I don't want to be the only female on their trip."

"I probably can't afford it."

"It'll be really cheap. We have a big van we are going to sleep in most of the time. You can save rent money," Ken said.

"Okay then. I'm in."

We found another girl from Hong Kong, so it became three female and three male.

Trip east

Of the three males on our trip, one was older with a wife at home. He was a new arrival so unfamiliar with everything. We called him Oldie. Another one was younger and also new. We called him Tiny. They were both small and skinny. The other Hong Kong girl was someone we found last minute. She was older, easy going and quiet. Ken was the natural top dog of the pack.

True to Ken's word, we slept in the van. The guys drove at night, we dozed off in the back. One guy was responsible for reading the map and keeping the driver awake, unless if Ken drove, then Malia sat in the front.

My seat was in the back behind the driver, so I got to enjoy my hobby of zoning out everything to zone in the scenery. But Ken would shout from the front, "Hey Konglong, don't fall asleep!" Konglong is dinosaur in Mandarin but Ken meant it to be Diplodocus, suggesting I could eat up all the vegetation on earth. They had discovered I ate as much as Oldie or Tiny. "At this rate you will be fat in a few months," Ken said. I just smiled. My mom always told me, "Eat! You are too thin."

Niagara Falls was our first stop. It was a "wow!" Boston was a "blah." Then we took the coastal route from Boston to New York.

"Hey stop, fresh strawberries!" Malia shouted.

We stopped and gorged on strawberries. Then fresh corn, then peaches.

"There should be a crab shack in a mile," Malia said.

It was the best stop for the six of us islanders - a long table covered with newspaper, freshly boiled crabs and potatoes spread out, we were given bibs and tools, but used our fingers and teeth to get at every little bit of meat in the nooks and crannies.

Lady Liberty, we took naps under her wing…

Those of us in the car had been kicked out of the house. Someone came by and said, "We have a priority-one meeting in fifteen minutes!" She then hurried down the street to tell others.

Priority-one meeting meant everyone must attend and dress appropriately. I opened my duffel bag in the trunk of our car. A sour sweat smell emanated. "Oh no! I haven't washed my clothes. I have nothing to wear!" …

"Konglong wake up!" Ken pulled my ankle. I awoke to find myself on a bench somewhere in Liberty State Park. We had also slept on grassy lawns with our rolled up sweatshirt as pillows and jackets as blankets. I had drifted, from a charming fine lady to a homeless. The English finishing school was a complete waste on me.

Empire State Building was supposed to be romantic, but no one in our group knew why.

We drove by the Twin Towers. "So tall. What's it famous for?" I said.

"World trade, I suppose," Ken said.

The tour at Ellis Island made me pause and think. The land of the free was not always free to everyone. The Chinese and Japanese immigrants had been prejudiced against and even imprisoned. The photo of a wife reunited with her husband after his lock-up etched into my mind. Of course Oldie and Tiny didn't help our image. They swiped towels and toilet paper from hotels, the few nights when we did sleep in hotel rooms.

By the end of the the week long "ride a fast horse to look at flowers" trip, I was exhausted. In the back seat while zoning out, Ken said, "Konglong, even if your specie becomes extinct, you would survive…"

I was sitting in a straight back seat in a wide hallway. My friend was sitting across from me. My other friend came and sat down next to her and they started talking. Then they got up and went around the corner. I followed. We sat on an elevated platform against a wall. They lay down on their sides to talk face to face. I scooted close to my friend and sat with my back against the wall.

"My ankle hurts," she said.

He said nothing, so I butt in, "I noticed that." She looked up at me as though I said something stupid. Next thing I know, my friend wanted to divorce me.

"Draw up the paper, I'll sign," I said.

My friend was in the driver seat. I was in the middle of the backseat looking out the front window and at her back. Tears welled up in my eyes…

First love

School started as soon as we got back to Madison. My kitchen-turned-dorm-room was in Chadbourne Hall. It had a bunk and a twin bed. The bunkbed was in front of the window making the room dark, and there was no desk, so everyone lingered in the TV room or the hallways, but I avoided those areas. "It's like a jungle there," I told Malia. Before bedtime my roommates shared stories. One told us about her sorority rush, "I was blind folded and had to drink something disgusting. At least it's not pee," she flashed her buck teeth, her eyes bulging. My other roommate was Jewish. She came back one day with her naturally wavy hair cut in layers. The two of us were envious. "It's like natural Farrah Fawcett hair!" The talk turned to beauty tricks. Buck Teeth brought out a blush compact and lipsticks. "You should try this lipstick with this blush," they told me. Then one day, the Jewish girl didn't come back. My buck teeth roommate said, "The girls down the hall accused her of stealing. She couldn't take the pressure and dropped out."

Yoko and Sally had also left after summer. Meanwhile Malia asked me to take Music In Performance. "You just need to show up. No homework. No exams." "Use the time to nap." "They need audience for the music majors." "It's worth one credit of electives." I signed up. The rest of my subjects were Calculus 2, Chemistry 1 and General Physics.

During Chemistry, my worse subject, I reminisced about the trip out east, and Ken. "I think I love him," the thought kept coming up, "why not tell him? I think he would like to hear it."

So I invited Ken to the fountain just outside Memorial Library. "I think I'm in love with you," I told him plainly, looking at the ground. I don't remember his response that day, something like "you just miss my teasing." But the next day he called me, "Want to meet me at the fountain after class?" Of course I agreed. That afternoon, a warm and sunny day, I sat on the edge of the fountain, water splish-splashed behind me. Ken showed up carrying a plastic bag with a red W logo. In it was a small stuffed tiger in yellow stripes.

"You like it?"

"I love it!"

"You want to study with me?"

Just like that Ken and I started studying together at the Memorial Library. Soon we started kissing in one of the many enclosed cubicles. Then we started groping each other. Then we went to Ken's apartment where he shared with Oldie and Tiny. When they saw us, they shook their heads. Then we went into Ken's room. "Stop," Ken said. I stopped. He was always the one who set the limit. He was the one who stopped the long kisses, where the groping went. He would not let us go beyond kissing and touching, and always fully clothed.

So I had to mention Ken to my mom and dad, casually, "Mom you don't have to worry about 'alien' parties and drugs. I only went to one. It was boring and I haven't been since. I already know a lot of people, so rather spend time with them than to parties. Right now I'm spending more time with a boy from Singapore. He is not good looking but a nice person, witty but grounded and honest. He encourages me to study hard, goes with me to libraries, etc. You don't be too sensitive. We are just friends."

October 1, 1982

Dear Baba, Mama, Aunt Shan,

Just received your letter. Can't believe Baba's one letter, already six big lectures. But I have read it a few times already, and agree they make good sense.

About majoring, I still haven't decided. At first I thought my Chemistry was weak, so I worked extra hard and got 95%. But the day after Chemistry was Physics test. Originally I had high confidence in Physics, so didn't prepare much, but put all my time on Chemistry, so my Physics test score ended up with 55%, barely a B. But my homework scores were good, teaching assistant gave me high scores. Math is the same, no problems, got 100% in the test!

I heard Hong Kong will return to China in 17 years. If so Chemical Engineers will be useful in China and America, right? I still don't want to study Chemistry. Just want to point this out. As for which one I pick, I'll know after this semester is over. Someone suggests I study Civil Engineering. What do you think?

I will keep up with letters to Higgins and Cayton. I'm still waiting for their reply to my last letters. I forgot if they have my new address.

Received Fai's letter. I feel like he has become much more obedient. He has settled down and started studying hard. From Min's letter, I know his school is quite good, down to earth and with few Chinese. It seems not easy for him to have bad influence. My understanding is when students just arrive in England, their English is not good, not easy to make English friends, so then they spend most of the time studying. Maybe Fai is in the same situation. At least he replied the day after he received my letter. When he was at home, I could not expect him to do the same.

Is it really quiet at home now? Aunt Shan saying she wants to quit? I hope she would stay.

Will Didi and Min return to Hong Kong for Christmas? Uncle Manuel sent me a postcard from California. He will return to Mexico, but did not leave me an address. So then is he, Grandpa and Grandma Cuan still at the same address in Mexico? Where should I send their letters to? Uncle Manuel said Big Cousin wants me to visit them for Christmas, but I've already promised Aunt Kay to to visit them, so won't go to California.

As for making friends, I know quite a few Hong Kong students, but not well. I discovered most of them are typical Hongkongers, very materialistic. Most of them own cars, don't know if they are really wealthy or of the kind who have no qualms spending family money once they come overseas. They only go to classy restaurants. When I go out with them, I have to dress up, too much trouble, so I avoid them whenever possible. The Singapore friends I went out east with are also wealthy, but not as materialistic as the bunch of Hongkongers. They have more righteous thinking, especially the one I know well. He teaches me how to be a person. He said I don't seem to have any goals, not steady and not grounded. Although he is not a saint himself. His only goal is to go home and help with his father's business. His father has business in Indonesia, but is getting old, so he wants to help him.

Anyway, won't write anymore. Hope Baba has time will write more. I love listening to your opinion. Your critical thinking is much better than mine. Now that I know Mama has help looking at slides, and has more free time, I'm relieved. Hope you won't argue over Mama's work anymore.

That's all. I'm very well. Wish all of you at home with good health.

Respectively,

Hiu-ha

October 1, 1982

First breakup

I saw Malia less and less. It was no secret everyone knew Ken and I were going together.

When we strolled around campus, Ken would point out some of the well known Asian beauties to me. There was one from Shanghai, one from Singapore, two from Vietnam and one from Korea.

"You could be as beautiful as them if you put on some makeup," Ken said.

Makeup was one beauty tip I did not learn in England. It was not allowed in my boarding school. None of my friends, not even Michelle was into makeup. Michelle taught me to apply Oil Of Olay twice a day, that was the extend of my beauty regime.

I studied myself. My curls had grown out with some waves remain. I had it cut to shoulder length with thick bangs. My wardrobe contained Gloria Vanderbilt tight jeans, dark color dress pants; unicolor loose fitting boxy or hang-off-the-shoulders t-shirt tops, sweatshirts, sweaters and an army green oversize padded jacket. My only fitted top, my favorite, was an army green cotton blazer. Summer was long loose skirts and my English school uniform - straight cut dresses of various shades of blue.

Then I studied Ken, big and heavy with a pudgy face and square glasses. I ignored his makeup suggestion. Just before Christmas break, I had had enough of my wavy hair. Short hair had become fashionable with the kind of girls I respected, so I had mine cut short, a boy cut, all without consulting Ken. When he saw me, he was visibly abhor. "What did you do to your hair!" Even Oldie and Tiny did not approve. "You look like a boy," they said.

Then we all went home for Christmas break, me Hong Kong, the others Singapore.

When we returned in January. Ken called me on the phone. He said, "I want to take a little break."

"What? Why?" I refused to believe him. I had been looking forward to seeing him again and even imagined taking a vacation with him somewhere, just him and me, to the House On The Rock or the Dells.

"I need to concentrate on school work. I have tough classes this semester."

January snow falling outside my dorm window, my first Wisconsin winter was bitter cold. I started crying on the phone.

Then Malia called me, "He really just need to study hard this semester." "Just wait and see what happens after finals." "You know what, there are three scholars from Singapore this year. You want to meet them?"

"No thank you."

I called Ken on the phone and cried again. "Don't cry. Please don't cry. Why are you crying?"

Somehow I got through the next few days by throwing myself into studying. And then I started transporting myself to California. I applied for summer school at UC Berkeley, made plans to visit Grandpa Grandma Cuan, Uncle Manuel and Cousin David. They were moving to LA from Mexico that summer, when my mom and dad would also go visit. Polly, a mutual friend of Maria and I from our high school days in Hong Kong, wrote that she would be in Los Angeles as well. We arranged to meet up. I continued writing to Maria and Yit, but not to the Kwok sisters and Katie because they did not write me back, not even once. I spent more time in Witte Hall with Bonnie my American dorm-mate, who was often in the room. I joined the Hong Kong Student Group to learn Chinese dance, but instead learned I had no talent. The rest of the semester flew by. Deep down I was still sure Ken wanted me back, but not sure I wanted him back anymore.

3

Summer 1983 Part 1

Summer came as a hot whirlwind. I started in a LA suburb with my Cousin Kwan and his family of wife and two small boys, then on to Grandpa Grandma Cuan's new place. Uncle Manuel treated me and Cousin David to Universal Studios and Disneyland. From there I met up with Polly. We went with her two male friends and drove up to Berkeley. Of the two friends, the better looking one was Polly's boyfriend. Both of them were our age, fun loving and appeared to be from wealthy families. All three were going for summer school at UCLA.

At UC Berkeley, I sublet a room in a house with two girls. On my daily walk to classes on Telegraph Avenue, I couldn't help but wondered about all the homeless people on the avenue.

"They all sleep in People's Park," my housemates told me. "Dropouts who can't handle the pressure and went nuts." "Some jumped off the Sather Tower."

Students under stress who jumped off towers or shot professors were not uncommon. But the homeless might have realized something else... "We don't need know education. We don't need no thought control..."

June 20, 1983

Min,

It took so long to get a decent letter from you. Now that your exams are over, you must be relaxed all over! I'm studying Linear Algebra and Statics, doing well, think I can get A's. Actually since I came for summer school, I only need to pass, because grades won't get transferred back to Wisconsin. Berkeley is not as intense as I imagined. Maybe summer school is easier. I want to transfer here, but don't know what major. I know I won't get into Electrical Engineering here, and I refuse to major in Chem E. I just can't study Chem. Chem to me has no logic, I have to memorize. But for people who like Chem, it doesn't need memorization, it can be reasoned out, but I just don't know how to reason it out.

Right now I'm living in an apartment, flatmate is from Hong Kong. Another girl is from Japan, but born in the US. Right now I cook my own meals. Here is a Hi-Fi, TV, not bad. Polly also came to study summer school. I meet her often to tour around.

After summer school I can stay here a few more days. Easy to buy plane tickets to LA and not expensive. I can wait until Mom and Dad get here before booking flights. I already phoned Uncle. He said I can go anytime.

A few days ago I wrote to ask Dad to buy a programmable calculator. Can you ask Mom to find that letter? It has details of what I want. Also can you buy me George Lam's new tape? And the Laura - Les sommes de l'ete I told you before. If there are any good songs at home, record for me. As for clothes, you can decide which ones. Can ask Didi for help. Attached pictures can give you some idea, but no need to buy the exact ones, cheap ones will be fine. Whatever you get, get me the same. No pants. Buy casual skirts and tops okay. Shirt size waist 26 inches. Tops the bigger the better. If it fits you, buy it. I haven't gotten fat or thin, still the same as Christmas time when I was home. Color best to be white, black, blue, light grey, pink and light purple.

Okay, all for now. Will write again when Mom and Dad get here.

Sis.

June 20, 1983

Summer 1983 Part 2

Polly and her friends came to visit most weekends. We went to Lake Tahoe, rented a boat for a day, drove around San Francisco. After summer exams we drove south to Hoover Dam and Las Vegas before they dumped me off with Grandpa and Grandma Cuan in their new home, where I met up with Mom and Dad.

The first thing Dad said to me was, "How did you get an F in Programming Language?"

My report card was sent home before I had a chance to see it myself.

"F? The class was full, I didn't even get in!" I was on the waiting list, but the professor told me I would not make it in, so I never attended the class. "I'll sort it out when I get back." Only then did Dad slackened up on me.

Last days of summer, Polly went to Columbia University. Her friends stayed at UCLA. My dad went north to Stanford University where he would start his one year residency. I went back to Madison. This time I didn't have lingering feelings towards the boys, even after our good times together.

Fall 1983

In the fall, my dorm-mate Bonnie, her friend Colleen and I moved into an apartment together. This was a big improvement from the converted kitchen-dorm-room at Chadbourne with two other girls, to a real dorm with one roommate in Witte, to now my own private room in a shared apartment on South Brooks Street on the south east part of campus. It was a long walk to classes, the lake and shopping, but cheap and quiet.

I finally decided against Chemical Engineering and enrolled in Electrical Engineering.

To get into Engineering School meant I had to take harder classes like Modern Physics and Computer Programming. Pressure was starting to mount.

Dad calling from Stanford checking on me didn't help. "How was your test?" "You make the choice, you have to face it."

I would get him back. "What are you making for dinner?" "A week of leftovers can't be good" He told me he added fresh vegetables to his leftover every day. "You got a bike? Be careful." He didn't want to buy a car just to move around campus.

Meanwhile Malia kept bringing up Bei, one of the three Singaporean scholars. One day when he came into the cafeteria where Malia and I and another girl from Singapore were eating. The girl whispered, "He's really good looking for a scholar."

The other two scholars were short and thin, wore thick glasses, shoulders a little hunched forward. Bei was tall and slim and carried himself upright. His eyes were slanted and wore small rounded John Lennon glasses. I didn't like his face. "I'll never date him," I told myself. But then I started to run into him more often in different study areas. When he eventually asked me, "Do you want to go watch

WarGames with me?" I could not say no. He asked in a way that did not expect me to reject, yet completely sincere. Besides I liked movies. What could possibly happen?

Bei

I don't know what happened. I don't even remember our first kiss. Soon everyone treated us as a couple. And we started going together. Bei was only a year older than me. As a "scholar," he didn't have to go through Singapore's mandatory two year military training. We spent most of our times in the EE or Comp Sci study area, where other Singapore or Hong Kong students congregated.

"You can ask him for help now," Malia told me as soon as she found out I was with Bei.

"I'm still doing okay." I said. The truth was I liked the thrill of solving problems myself. You know the feeling when someone yells out an answer just before you were about to figure it out? I hated that.

Except one time, I was working on the Bubble Sort Algorithm for my programming class. We were in a open space on a large table in the basement of Comp Sci building. Under fluorescent lights, books, notebooks, paper scattered all over. Bei was across from me, other Asian engineering students around me. I stared at my computer printout.

"When I assign B to A, what's in A got wiped out. How am I supposed to swap them?" I muttered.

"Ugh!" I threw my pencil down.

"You need a third variable," Bei said, eyes on his book, barely lifted his head.

"Huh? I still don't get it. How would that help?"

Bei then gave me a look that suggests, "If you don't get it, you are not going to make it through engineering school."

My head dropped back down. This was supposed to be simple, according to the others around me, but they wouldn't help if Bei was there.

In those days computer times were limited and had to be reserved. For us engineering students, we had to let the Computer Science majors pick the slots first. This meant most of the leftover time-slots were from 1 AM to 5 AM, way past my bedtime. As such, I tried to do all my work on paper so I could get in and get out of the Comp Sci building as fast as possible. Before the Bubble Sort, my programs ran after one or two compiles, but this time it wouldn't. I had to come out into the open air to think. The computer room was suffocating with rows and rows of box shaped monitors and reams and reams of paper. Programming itself was not depressing to me. I loved to see logic proven by a computer.

I chewed my pencil, I scratched my head and studied the printout over and over. My confidence was down in the pits. After many scribbles and scratches, I wrote, "A, B, C." "C=A." "A=B," "no," "yes," "A=B." "B=A," no "B=C." "Yes! I got it!"

"Let me see," Bei checked it over and then nodded.

If he had explained in a different way, I could have understood it quickly. For example, he could have said, "Think of A and B as two bags of rocks." Then I might have thought of using another empty bag C. I could use C to hold A's rocks, so I could pour B's rocks into A, and then C into B. Even a crow can figure it out. But on paper, away from the real world and with abstract variables A, B, C, most people would be stumped. Bei was too intelligent to explain in layman's term, as are most professors and their assistants.

After that, I stopped asking Bei for homework help. I did not want him to look down on me the way he did. Besides when we studied together, he entered into a different world, and I was blocked out. When tests were over, he would emerge and became full of life. I would then fall in love with him all over again.

Our Friday date night was Chinese food and a movie. University Square had both - Shanghai Noodles and Mann Theater. Shanghai Noodles's owner's daughter was one of the Asian beauties. China was still closed to the rest of the world, so she was uniquely beautiful as the only one from China.

One night, the only decent movie at the theater was The Shinning. "Let's do something else. I don't like horror movies," I said.

"What's to be afraid of? I'm with you." Bei convinced me.

During the movie, when Jack Nickelson's character was typing away on the typewriter, Bei whispered, "He's typing garbage."

When later it was revealed that Jack was typing "all work and no play makes Jack a dull boy" over and over again, I looked over at Bei, awestruck, "How did you know?"

"Shh, watch."

In a later scene, when a red "redrum" was painted on the door, Bei said, "That says 'murder'."

"Oh yeah! Are you sure you haven't seen it before?"

"This is my first time, honest."

I believed him and admired him then. He was not only book smart, he was movie smart too!

One day I found a Playboy magazine in Bei's room. "Why are you reading Playboy?"

"I'm just curious. We don't get magazines like Playboy in Singapore."

'Which article do you like?"

"This one," flip, flip, "and this one."

I read them and thought they were no big deal. I had read similar ones in boarding school, but from women perspective.

Another time, Bei and a group of guys from Singapore were going to an XXX movie, showing in a classroom on campus.

"I'm going. You want to come with?" Bei said.

"Yes, If you go, I'm coming with."

The room was packed and there were few other females. I remember one specific scene when a man and a woman were crawling on a table full of food, stuffing and smearing each other with ripe fruits, soft cakes and drumsticks. At some point, everyone cheered.

Somehow all that did not change my view of Bei or the other Singaporeans at the XXX movie. I knew in Singapore they could not chew gum, would get flogged if they spray-paint graffiti. Now that they had the freedom to explore, it seemed completely harmless. They guys knew me and did not treat me any differently after the movie.

The first time Bei hurt me was when he didn't want to kiss me or even hug me after he received an A minus in a final.

"What's wrong? Don't you love me anymore?"

"I don't even love myself, how can I love you."

"I have B's and C's, what's the big deal with A minus?"

"It means I no longer have a 4.0 GPA."

A small warning signal might have come to me then. "He cares more about his grades than me. Soon he will care about his career more than me." But the warning got buried. We had already gone too deep, having taken a road trip to Florida, and another one to Montreal

Canada, where Bei had spent a year before transferring to Madison. We told all the hotel check-in staff we were husband and wife.

Summer 1984 Part 1

That whole school year my world was just Bei, and occasionally Bei's friend and his American girlfriend. This girlfriend majored in Chinese and had advanced to reading Chinese literature. I had not stayed in touch with her, but quite sure I saw her on TV in Beijing interviewing a Chinese witness after the "incident" at Tiananmen Square on June 4th 1989.

I was rarely home. Ken called Bei a pretty boy, so we avoided him and Malia. Colleen my housemate complained heavily of me not cleaning the bathroom and the kitchen. My response was that I hardly use the apartment, never cooked in the kitchen. Bonnie defended me and often did my share. When our one year lease ended, Bonnie and Colleen renewed theirs, but I moved to a one-room apartment which was just a large room with its own door lock, and a shared bath with four another tenants, in a charming Victorian house in a quiet neighborhood on Adams Street on the south side of campus, closer to Engineering School. To reduce rent, I agreed to clean the bathroom. "Can't stand the dirty bathroom, might as well get paid to clean it," I reasoned.

Then Bei broke the news, I barely settled into my new place, "I got the internship in Minneapolis!"

"Oh! Great." "But I have summer school." I had taken too many filler electives such as French to offset the intense engineering classes, so then had to attend summer school to stay within the four year program.

A week after Bei settled in Minneapolis, I took the Greyhound bus to see him.

"Wow you get this whole apartment to yourself?"

It was the biggest and the most upscale apartment I'd seen so far -

clean, fully equipped kitchen and light oak furniture - all provided by his company. I wanted to visit him every weekend to explore Minneapolis, where I had not been before. The following week on the phone, Bei told me he was busy that weekend, and the following weekend, and the one after that. "Try to find something to fulfill yourself besides me," he said.

Suddenly I was all alone.

My summer courses were Machine Language Programming and EE Lab 1, both easy. Plus Tennis as elective.

At that time, my leisure reading was a book by a Chinese author about her daily life on a farm in Utah with her American husband. I loved her style enough I thought I could write like her. "It'll fill up my weekends without Bei," I decided. With a new notebook, on the sloped lawns by Lake Mendota or outdoor tables at the Memorial Union, I started writing.

First essay

July 23, 1984, Monday 3 PM

Bei left. I stayed at school for summer classes by myself. When classes are done, there is nothing to do. All day I think of Bei. At night when I speak with him on the phone, I can't avoid pouring out my troubled heart. Bei hears it so much, he becomes impatient. Maybe Bei is right. If I can't even absorb this little separation, what will I do in the future? Bei will graduation soon. Won't I be left alone here then? On top of that, life is full of leave leave and together together. I should learn to accept this reality. Bei, he misses me too, but he is stronger than me. When he uses all his strength to find things to do to fulfil himself, then days go by easily. Thinking and thinking, I start to deeply hate my weakness. I have to be like Bei, learn to enjoy the joy of aloneness.

So then, my days have become busy again. Every morning, tennis. After school, bicycle, to the lake I go. Under tree shades I sit, hours go by. Looking and looking at the calm calm water, distance sails in dots upon dots, sometimes one or two speed boats pulling athletic skiers ride by with the wind. Without aware, time flown by and are gone. I also like to go on the streets, to check out the beautiful shop window displays, to study people of all colors and shapes - some dress like flower branches waving and reaching out, some one of a kind, an armor of punk, the younger ones three or five a cluster, walking, laughing. I don't know when a street full of merchants flowed here. Those sell things, those sell clothes, those sell eats, they fill the wide wide street so water cannot even leak through. Under the shower of summer sun, Madison State Street is so full of the putt putt breaths of life. The winter cold emptiness all brushed away. Everyday I linger here, amazingly, days pass much quicker.

Although sometimes, that empty lost heart feeling still floats up and shows itself. Bei said it's because my life has no purpose. I only know one day goes by, then another. He seems to be right again. The shape of my future is buried in the fog with me. Be an ordinary housewife? My heart won't rest. My study is engineering. Although I have interest in engineering, I'm not in love with it. Because science is dead, without emotions. I often dream to be an artist, or a musician, or a dancer, but I don't have the talent. Last night on my bed, I turned, stretched and couldn't sleep. Suddenly I thought of writing. Writing does not need talent. If you have something to say, you can write. Question is if anyone wants to read your words. No matter what, it is not a dead end. I have always liked read read and write write. It's just I've never seriously written anything good. As long as I start practice now, it's not too late, for sure.

I didn't think that today I would really buy this notebook. I decided from now on, I'll write something everyday. I really have to fill this thick thick book. If there is a chance, I'll share with others about my thoughts, and the sights and sounds I've seen.

Third essay

July 26, 1984

I don't like Hongkongers. Hongkongers don't like me. They say I am a Singaporean, or half white. I know what they think. They think I stick with Singaporeans because when Hong Kong returns to China, I can go to Singapore. Small hearted people. I don't want to go to Singapore. If I don't want to go back to Hong Kong, I can easily stay in America. They think everyone is like them who wants to leave Hong Kong.

I don't like Hong Kong people's materialism. A guys has a green card, family has some money, hands on a car, is like the world is his, thinks all the girls of the world would fall down and worship him. Every chance they get, they show off their wealth. They tell people which high class place they have been, where they go on holidays. I met a guy. The second time I went out to dinner, he asked me right away for my plans when Hong Kong returns to China. He then started his speech, something something he has Canadian citizenship; he doesn't have to open his mouth, his family sends him money every month. The amount he gets a month is enough for my whole year's expense. His place has video recorder, computer, not to mention his luxury car. Our nice dinner is spoiled, the food can't even go down my throat. Next time, I avoid him for my own luck. If I have to listen to him to count his possessions again, I'll go crazy.

Another poor guy, his family is not rich, but tries to pretend he is rich. With his hard earned money, he buys a car. Then he goes everywhere to show off. Unfortunately it's costly to buy a car, it is even more costly to take care of the car. The monthly insurance, gas, repairs and maintenance, all add up to a big amount. Where would he get so much money? Then I notice him in and out of the cafeteria. Turns out he is working there to earn money for his car, which is fine. But after a car, he wants a computer. Eventually news broke out that someone stole a computer. He got caught red handed. What I write here is all true.

Of course Hongkongers are materialistic. Taiwanese are also materialistic. So are Singaporeans. Except I met many annoying Hong Kong materialistic guys, but one lovely Singaporean. Bei often admits he is materialistic. He says he lives for money. Bei's family is poor. If not for the scholarship, he won't ever make enough money to study abroad. Actually Bei is not that poor now. His sponsoring company sends him money for living expenses and textbooks. His income is more than a lot of people. But his place is so tiny, it's pitiful. From the door, one step gets me to the bed. From the bed, half a step to the desk. From the desk, half a step gets me to the door again. In his room, there is nothing but books in every corner. I had to even force him to buy a curtain. He said, "What's wrong with no curtain? In the morning, the sun wakes me up. At night, the moon sleeps with me." He kills me. I laugh that his room is like a cabin in a boat, but he just doesn't care. Until one day I was making coffee in his room. In this small small room I turned and turned looking for sugar, for coffee ground, for power outlet. Once I opened the drawer, once I moved the chair, there was no more room for me to turn. Coffee got spilled. My head bumped the bookshelf. The whole room got turned upside down. Only then, for the first time, he realized his room was tiny.

Where does all his money go? One time I went shopping with him. We saw stylish menswear and home decorations I asked him to buy, but he had no interest. Except in the book store and electronic store where he spent half a day. All he bought were books. He also likes to travel. Each holiday costs him hundred of dollars to a rent car. On my birthday, he bought a bouquet of roses, two big teddy bears, and treated me to a big dinner. His money is unknowingly and unawarely spent like this.

I say Bei is materialistic because he says his only goal in life is to make lots of money. He wants to be a multi-millionaire. He honestly admits he is poor and he is "crazy for big fortune." But with his blunt personality, he won't know how to enjoy his money.

"What good is all that money?" I asked him.

He replied without hesitation, "It's for throwing at people."

I didn't understand. He explained that in this realistic world, people don't care if you are capable. No matter how much you know, how good a heart you have, people only care about your money, your clothes, your house, your car. The more money you have, the more friends you have, everyone pays you respect by thousands of degree. If you don't have money, people won't even lift a corner of their eyes at you.

Bei is prideful, competitive, intelligent, earns top ranks at school; but without money, people ignore him. There are others whose families have money, their grades not that good, but they easily enter well-known universities. This is why he wants to make a lot of money, to throw money at each of them who looks down on him. He wants to prove he does not need to depend on his parents. He wants to make money with his own two hands. He wants to mock those who are arrogant and ignorant.

I bless him in my heart. I hope he succeeds. I hope he won't let his own money throw him down.

A vent

(This was written in English, and then all the rest of my meager journal entries became English, while all my letters were in Chinese.)

August 2, 1984

Why do you hurt me so much? I was thinking of you, missing you, and I was wondering if you felt the same way too. I wanted to talk to you, but it was only 9:00 PM. So I waited for two hours. After 11, I picked up the phone to call you. When your familiar voice came through the phone, I could not help the happiness I felt in me. After all, you are home, you're not sleeping, and there you are at the end of the line. You sounded indifferent, you did not seem particularly happy about me calling, you did not seem to want to talk. I did not mind holding the phone like that, without talking, just to know that you're there is good enough. But I know you don't like it, you will be angry at me if I don't say something. You told me you hated it. So I desperately made conversation, I asked you about your work, not knowing you are not happy about it. So we went on for an hour. You complained, I consoled. I don't know if you appreciate me calling or not, I don't know if you want to talk to me about those things or not. Maybe you prefer to be left alone. Maybe you prefer to carry on with your report, your TV, or whatever else you were doing. But I went on, we went on, because I haven't heard the thing I wanted to hear yet. I heard no sign that you miss me, that you are thinking of me, that you've wanted to call me too. I should not have expected too much, but I did. As usual you finally lost your temper. You started to shout at me. You wanted me to hang up the phone. You hurt me. You did everything you could to get me off the phone, so that you can have some peace. Do you know how much that hurts? What am I? A cheap, miserable little girl begging for affection, begging for a little love? That's what I was. You don't have much to offer do you? Fuck you Bei. You hurt me. You tear my heart to pieces, you glue them back together when you feel like it, just so you can tear it apart again. You don't understand me. You never will. I don't understand you either. I don't know the cold cruel you. I don't know when you'll turn into that animal again. I don't know when you feel like being nice to me. How I hate you. How I hate you cheated me. You made me believe you were true to me, that you truly loved me. And let me find out all these ugly sides of you only now, after all these good times we've had. What am I to do now? It's so easy for you to break up a relationship. You just turn around and walk away, as easy as that, and leave me bleed to death on the floor. You're such a self-centered creep. All you ever care about is your work, your study, your reports, your paper, your programs. You are busy, forever busy. No one in the world can be busier than you. I have programs too, reports too, final exams too. But my busyness is nothing compare to yours. You're a born busy man. You're great. I'm nothing. I can flunk all my courses. It doesn't matter. But you cannot get a B. You don't give a damn if I don't do well. But you get angry if someone does not appreciate you. Your world is made of success, achievements, work, jealousy, hate, work and more work. My world is simple, not particularly great, but okay. But now there is only misery and hurt. Sorry I am discouraging you again, because I am jealous of you, of what you have achieved. Everybody is jealous of you. Everybody use you. I go out with you because you are so smart, because you are rich (in the future). Yes I'm jealous. I don't want you to be successful. I only want to slow you down. So that you will be a nobody. Everybody is against you, including me. You are at the top of the world, alone. You are the greatest. Bei the greatest.

Please think about it. Do I love you or hate you? Do you think it's possible that I become jealous of you? What is there to be jealous about? Why don't you trust anyone? Why do you take something I say so literally, twist it into bad intentions?

Please don't hurt yourself and hurt me. I don't know how much more I can take.

Bonnie went home this weekend. She left while I was at class. When I came back, I saw a note on the table, with a little flower she plucked somewhere. The note wished me a good weekend. She's just a girl I share this apartment with, who I occasionally talk to. I never care for her one tenth as much as I care for you. But here she is, telling me in the simplest way that she appreciates me. What about you? Why do you always make me feel that I'm a nuisance to you, that you'd be better off without me, that you'd be much more successful without me to discourage you?

Summer 1984 Part 2

It didn't take long for my social life to pick up again. I met Tenia, another Singaporean, to play tennis with. Then I got to know her circle of friends - Singaporeans who were not poor, but not wealthy, kind of like me. They liked to have fun, and I joined them. My writing notebook got put on a shelf and neglected.

At the end of the summer, Bei returned from his internship as he was before. I welcomed him back with half opened arms. I had enjoyed my new friend circle, and wanted Bei to be a part of that. Bei had no interest whatsoever. He was applying to grad school and needed to study seriously. I relented and we resumed our old routine, again mostly by ourselves.

September 29, 1984

Dear Baba, Mama,

How are you? Just received your letter, very happy. The whole summer I only got a couple of letters from Min. All along I didn't know if all is well at home, so I'm extra happy now that I got your letter. Classes have started for almost a month. Homework keeps me very busy. This semester I'm taking five courses - Lab, Computer Numerical Methods, three EE courses (Fields & Waves, Electromagnetic Circuits, Signal and Systems), all very hard stuff. This is why I'm very busy. New house is very nice. It's near Engineering Building, close to all my classes. Rent is cheaper. $180 per month, $20 cheaper than before. New phone number is 608-251-0709. Weekday night after 8 PM I will for sure be home. I study at home everyday. It is more quiet, easier to concentrate. Everything else is going very well.

From your letter it seems Fai's problem is still the same as before. I think if Baba is really worry about Didi, you might have to change your lecture method. I'm not helping Mama, but Baba lectured me the same way when I was still living at home, so I can understand Didi's thinking. Baba your tone is sometimes too serious, pushing people into a corner. Even though you are right, it is difficult to take it. If you are fierce at the onset, I just won't listen. Didi definitely won't. You can't let him know you are lecturing him, have to slowly influence him. When you used to blow up on us, I had always wanted you to calm down and listen to what we have to say and let us explain. If you get angry easily, we will only try to escape, instead of wanting to change. I know Didi knows he needs to work hard, but without the perseverance needed to overcome his laziness. It's best Baba and Mama change positions. Baba be more gentle. Mama be more strict. The result would be much better.

I'll tell Didi too. More importantly let him come home at Christmas. Then I can talk to him face to face. He must have changed a lot in the last two years. Plus he never writes me. I don't even know what's on his mind. I've checked the tickets, but haven't booked yet. Roughly come home December 24 or 25, because exams don't finish until the 22nd.

That's all. This semester I may not write much, because I'm really really busy. Don't even have time to do laundry. Every week there is lab report due, like ten sheets or more. Have to write computer programs, plus meetings and so on. Let's talk when I get home.

Wish all is well. Say hi to Aunt Shan for me.

Respectfully,

Hiu-ha

September 28, 1984

Christmas 1985

For Christmas break, I was going home. Bei was going to Singapore. Hong Kong was an easy extra stop on Bei's way home. Besides, he had never been to Hong Kong. I could show him around. So I told my parents about Bei, even sent them a photo, and arranged for him to stayed with us for two days. Mom and Dad were eager to meet him.

My brother Fai was home that Christmas as well, but Min remained in London. She was in her second year of Civil Engineering at Imperial College.

Our first meal home was at my parents' flat in Baguio Villa where I spent my pre-teen years. Mom, Dad, Fai, Bei and I sat around our circular table overlooking Telegraph Bay.

"Can't believe they filled the waterfront and put up new highrises," I said.

"The rocks where we fished off of are gone," Fai said.

"The swimming pool and playground still look the same."

"Eat, eat," Mom said in Mandarin while placing steamed chicken and Bokchoi into Bei's bowl. "You graduate next year?"

"Yes, going to Berkeley."

"Where did all these people come from?" I said.

"The Brits trying to squeeze more out of Hong Kong before handing it back to China," Fai said.

"What do you know," Dad said. Turning to Bei, he said, "Did you apply to Stanford?"

"Stanford is kind of expensive." Bei was rejected by Stanford and MIT.

"They give out many scholarships."

"Didi you need to gain some weight. Your eyes are sunk in."

"Eat. More tea?"

"Stanford is snobbish," Fai said.

"I agree. Berkeley is more liberal," I said.

"Eat, eat. More?"

The next days, Mom pushed us out, "Go show Bei around." She tended to get stressed out with guests hanging around at home.

Fai and I showed Bei all the tourist spots - Victoria Peak, Star Ferry, Tsim Sha Tsui, Stanley Beach, Ocean Park. Fai, being Fai, was talkative and sociable. It became he and Bei talked while I absorbed the atmosphere and scenes. The three of us ate out the rest of the time. "I miss Wonton, let's go get some." Also meatballs on a stick, Dandan noodles, black pepper steak, salt fried shrimps, tea eggs, tomato cheese pork chop over rice bake, and more.

In a quiet moment by ourselves, Bei said, "I don't think your dad likes me." "You all talked without me."

"I'm sorry. I'm just excited to be home." "And with you."

"You are lucky. You family is so lively. I can see where your quick wit comes from."

"We all fight to talk."

"My family is too big." "I have nothing to talk to them about."

I realized I knew little about his family, other than his parents were old. He had many siblings. He was in the middle. He had an older brother in Canada. Not sure how his brother could afford to go to Canada, probably with scholarship.

"There's little to know," Bei had said, and I didn't care enough to probe.

After Bei left, Mom and Dad pulled me aside.

"He's not right for you," Dad cut to the point.

"Why? I thought you would love him. He's just like you. Intelligent, hard working, ambitious."

"We think it's too early for you to settle, but I like him," Mom said.

"He's too ambitious. I don't think he loves you all that much." Dad always had a way of aiming where it hurt.

"Is it because his family is poor? I didn't think you care about family background," I fought back.

"What happens when he goes to Berkeley?"

I did not reply. We put the argument aside. Dad knew then he did not have to worry all that much about Bei.

Fai and I each had our own friends to visit, but spent some time shopping together.

"What'd you think of Bei?"

He shrugged. "He's very smart. Knows a lot of different things." "You gonna marry him?"

"Haven't thought that far." "So tell me about your school."

He had been in England two and a half years already. "They call me Hilfred." "I'm on the field hockey team." "Some of my English friends live here in Hong Kong." "We hung out and smoke." His friends were all English because he was tall, he looked slightly caucasian, he was out-spoken, learned English fast and already sounded like a British. Like me, he had no hard boundaries, but unlike me, he did not enjoy studies.

I was supposed to help Dad lecture Fai, but instead we shared our mutinous stories. Our age gap was six years. After so many years apart and in three short weeks, we didn't reconnect, we rearranged our roles. I was no longer his nagging sister. We were more like fellow runaways. I told Dad, "Didi said he will work hard."

Dr. Higgins was also in Hong Kong for a short work trip at the HKU. He had been to Hong Kong a few times already, so Fai and I took him to the Big Buddha on Lantau Island. Mom and Dad treated him to dinner at the Jumbo Floating Seafood Restaurant.

On the way back to Wisconsin, Bei booked a hotel near Kai Tak Airport for one night. My parents thought I flew straight to Wisconsin. At the MTR subway station, I saw him in the line for tickets and slipped in front of him. "What's the matter? You seem cold," Bei said. He noticed I didn't flash him the usual big smile. I noticed he missed me more than usual.

The hotel room was newer and more expensive than the ones we had ever stayed at. On the queen size bed in the dark, Bei wanted to try penetration for the first time. He could not get in. I went down on him, also the first. Afterwards, I slipped into the bathroom and rinsed my mouth over and over again.

Bye Bei

Back in Madison that Spring semester of 1985, Bei and I resumed our routine, but more like study buddies than a couple. We both got buried in homework. I took two labs, plus Control Systems I, Nonlinear Electronic Circuits, Advanced Digital Systems, and Intro to Computer Architecture. Bei also had a full load like he always did. He was preparing for UC Berkeley. At the end of the semester, Bei graduated, so did Malia and Ken. I said goodbye to Bei in my heart because UC Berkeley would be out of reach for me for grad school, but we told each other to stay in touch. Before heading to Berkeley, Bei went home to Singapore. I went to Maryland to see Second Uncle and his family and stayed there for one week, then returned to Wisconsin for summer school.

July 1, 1985

Min,

Really happy to receive your letter. I'm getting less and less letters these days. Maybe it is because I'm writing less. I actually really want to come back to Hong Kong, especially after hearing you all went camping last summer. The only problem is the heat. This summer I'm only taking one class, technically it should be relaxing, but I still don't have enough time. Besides class, I'm now helping at the Engineering Department workshop. I don't get paid, because they already filled all the openings. But I desperately need working experience before graduate. So now work for no pay. At least next time if they hire, I will have a good chance. The work is not easy. I have to do soldering, put parts together and so on. In the afternoon, I go to school. Programming homework at night (I'm taking Computer Science). Luckily work and school goes only from Monday to Thursday. Friday to Sunday is free time. I'm usually by myself. My old girlfriends are all busy dating. I don't want to bother them. I sometimes go out with one or two of them, but it's not like before when I was always with someone.

It's actually not all that boring by myself. Last summer I bought a bicycle, so whenever I have free time I go ride around. There are many beautiful places here, all near where I live. Like now I'm sitting by the lake writing to you. This weekend is July 4th Independence Day. The U has a lot of activities. Student Association is hosting a party. At least I won't be bored this few weeks. Here I have answered all your questions.

(I haven't written a separate letter to Mom and Dad, but all I want to tell them is the same, so you can let them read this so they know how I'm doing.)

* * *

I didn't finish this letter last time. Now it's another few days. Yesterday was July 4th. Madison is the capital of Wisconsin, so every year there is fireworks. Yesterday I was at the lake watching fireworks.

What have you been doing at home these days? Is Second Cousin still there? Grandpa Grandma Cuan called me last week and told me Second Cousin went to Hong Kong. The two of them by themselves can be quite lonely, so they call me sometimes. Sometimes they send clothes and candies. The clothes don't usually fit me, but it shows their heart.

Tell you a little gossip. When I was at Second Uncle's house, Aunt Kay told me a lot of things. She is not getting along with Second Uncle. She wants to get a divorce, but because of their sons welfare, she doesn't dare to. Aunt Kay is very kind to me, but I feel she is in the wrong. She is the type who doesn't like to settle down. Her heart is younger than me, always want to go out and play. Second Uncle is more down to earth. Aunt Kay thinks he is boring. She thinks if she gets a divorce, then she can live the kind of life she wants. All in all it is trouble. I feel like now there are few couples who are happy together. My previous roommates (both American), both their parents are divorced. At the airport, I met a thirteen year old girl. Her parents got divorced, each married someone else, then they each got divorced again, then remarried each other, then they got divorced again. What a joke! Polly's older sister married an American, now they are divorced. If you have a boyfriend, you need to be extra careful to understand him! All these about uncle and Polly, please don't tell anyone else! Because this is other people's private business. If you tell Mom and Dad, tell them don't tell anyone else. Especially Polly's mom and dad.

Sis.

July 1, 1985

Free

When all the students came back from summer, Madison went into hyper party mode again. Party before football game, party after. Red and white covered the whole campus. Marching band mix mingled hard rock. "On Wisconsin!" "Might as well jump (jump)!" "Fight! fight, fight, we'll win the game." "On Wisconsin!" "Here I am. Rock you like a hurricane!" Beer and brat smell drifted out of every orifice, from Friday afternoon into early Sunday morning. Partiers reemerged from post apocalyptic frat-houses like zombies.

This was not the time to be alone. A couple of American engineering students asked me out, but they seemed too old or too geeky. I declined and thought, "Why is it only loser Americans ask Asians out?"

I tried harder to reach out to old friends. I hung out with my old roommate Bonnie, played tennis with Tenia from the previous summer. And then gradually I rejoined her circle of friends. This circle had rearranged itself over the past year. Tenia had a boyfriend. They were both from Singapore who were associated with the Singaporean beauty and her boyfriend who were associated with two Singaporean handsome guys who were associated with a Taiwanese beauty who was associated with a Taiwanese American who used to play high school football who was associated with a few Americans and the Korean beauty and a Thai beauty. All of a sudden, I was among the beautiful Asians group, which I nicknamed beauti-asians. Beautiful people only attract more beautiful people. Many were American citizens. English was our common language. At least half of the guys were engineering students. Of all the girls, only the Korean and the Thai wore makeup as a part of their daily outfit.

Our usual activity was cook and eat Thai food, Malaysian food,

Chinese food and American barbecue. We also ventured out to dances and football games. The Badgers football team was losing more than winning in those days, so the norm was to sneak into Camp Randal for the 5th Quarter marching band show, to jump and dance around on the bench seats to the tunes of Beer Barrel Poker, The Chicken Dance, and of course, to put our arms around each other and sway to You've Said It All.

Just like that, I dived off the straight and narrow bookshelf into the hot-mates pool. My grades dropped to B's and C's, and I fell off the Dean's List. Bei still telephoned me, "It's very competitive here," "I'm taking EE..."

4

The lab

The Engineering School programming lab was the size of a regular classroom, a fraction of the size of the Comp Sci computer center. I was sitting at a terminal trying to log-on to the Fortran Language system for the first time. My stomach was still queasy, stuffed with Malaysian Sambal and Rendang the night before. The programming assignment was due in a few days. I was already behind with the material in this Computer Project In Controls & Instrumentation course. The instructions on my homework sheet was scant. I managed to login, but the operating system was completely foreign to me. "How do I open a file?" Everyone around me was deep in concentration. As I struggled, my patience was running out. Then I looked up to see a lab assistant standing just outside the corner office, so up raised my hand. He came over and stood behind me. "I just need help navigating this OS. How do I open an edit session? It doesn't know 'vi.'"

"Use 'ed.'"

I typed "ed myProg" and an editor appeared.

"Oh it worked! Thank you."

"Let me get you a commands list." He disappeared and returned with a cheat sheet. "Compile, print, its all here."

"Thank you. This really helps."

"You need any more help I'll be in the office."

I got down to work typing in my code. Fortran was a new language to me and I was making more mistakes than if it were C or Pascal.

"You're still here?"

I looked up and noticed everyone had already left. "Er I'm almost done, just want to finish it today."

He sat down on the chair next to me. I noticed his ripped faded jeans and flannel shirt. This was beyond assistance. I became

100

uncomfortable and could no longer concentrate. He was sitting, which meant he was not leaving soon.

"Which class work is this?"

"Double E." I looked at his face for the first time, thick brows, clear blue eyes, soft cheeks tanned and lean, with short cropped brown hair. I saved the program and logged out.

"Got it working?"

"No, I'll come back tomorrow. Looks like this place is closing."

"Yes, I've already locked up the office."

Hastily, I stuffed my books and notebooks into my backpack. He stood and waited. We walked out together. The evening sun was soft. The entrance area deserted. Cars on University Avenue zipped by.

"So what year are you?"

"Senior."

"Senior, you don't look like a senior. Must be pretty smart to get to senior in double E."

We had reached the pedestrian path. I turned to my right. He stopped, so I had to stop.

"Are you married or seeing someone?"

He was an "alien," but not old, not geeky. "Not, married, I kind of have a boyfriend."

"Would you like to go out sometime?"

"Maybe, okay."

"What's your number? I'm Doug by the way."

"I'm Shirley. Mm, 251, 0709."

"Okay. Got it. I'll give you a call."

I turned in the direction of Union South, he towards the bike racks. He didn't write down my number.

No call

I floated in air to Union South. He asked if I was married! And he looked young, and kind of cute. I unlocked my bike. It rode me home. Dinner, I made pork chop with Cream of Mushroom soup and Chinese cabbage in an electric wok.

That night he didn't call, nor the next morning. Then I thought, "He didn't write down my number. Oh good. I can forget it. Something for me to brag about. No call no risk."

The next evening after classes, I went back to the lab to finish up my program. At the terminal, I rummaged around in my backpack for the cheat sheet. "Must have left it last evening trying to hurry out," I kicked myself. So I went to ask for another one. Just inside the office door, there he was, standing by the wall. *Shit.* I noticed right away his tight white jersey, the shape of his chest and shoulder muscles visible through the knit fabric. "I lost the cheat sheet," I said quickly, and then inaudibly, "really."

He handed me the sheet and said, "I have your number, but I was too busy to call. You still want to go out?"

"Mm. Sure."

It took only half an hour to finish up my program, and I left.

First date

That night, he called. "You free this Saturday?"

"Em yes."

"How about seven o'clock Saturday?"

Seven o'clock was past my dinner time, but I said, "Okay.'

"I can pick you up at your place." I gave him my address.

"Have you been to the bars on State Street?"

"Not really."

"I can show you a few. I'll call before I come over."

"Okay."

Saturday night, I put on a pair of black dress pants, a white shirt under a loose oversized yellow sweater. My long hair was held back with a plastic hairband. I pulled a few strands out to soften my high forehead. Seven o'clock, still no call. "What kind of a guy is late for a date?" Then seven fifteen. "Is he standing me up?" Seven thirty, my phone rang.

"I just finished my workout. Going to shower and change. I'll be over after that."

"Okay." No apology, no nothing. At least he explained why he was late.

The main door of my Victorian house was not locked. We met halfway on the stairs, I on my way down and he on his way up. He was wearing a two tone light weight suede jacket, faded jeans and cowboy boots, like someone walked right out of a movie. At the curb, a silver Buick was parked. He opened my side of the door and let me in.

"I didn't know you have a car. Most students don't have a car."

"I worked all summer for it." He drove with his left hand in his pocket, using his right palm to turn the steering wheel. I had never seen anyone drive like that. "Shouldn't he at least grip the wheel?"

Granted I couldn't drive yet. We passed the typical college bars like Kollege Klub. He drove farther east and parked near the State Capital.

At the first bar on a high stool round table, I sipped an orangy color drink. "It's Tequila Sunrise," he said. "It's sweet." "I thought you'd like it." I slammed it and started chewing the ice cubes. "You know, girls who chew ice cubes tend to be sexually deprived."

I ignored him. "How come you're new here and yet you're a senior?"

"I broke up with my girlfriend and needed a change of pace." He was a Math major transferred from Stevens Point Wisconsin. Before that he was in Santa Barbara. Before that he was in Western Michigan. He moved either because he needed money or broke up with a girlfriend. "My last girl friend cheated on me." "Madison is nice, but I don't fit in with the young crowd."

"You look to me like a typical American," which I only knew from movies. I was thinking Tom Cruise in Risky Business, they were even about the same height. Ice cubes crunched in my mouth.

"I'm not a typical American. I don't follow the herd."

I noticed his large forearm. "You like working out?"

"I was kind of fat around twelve, thirteen." "It's hard to get girlfriends if you're fat." His eyes twinkled, a small curve around his mouth. "I convinced my buddy to lift weights with me so I could lose some weight. Then I got into bodybuilding."

"Bodybuilding?"

"You finished with the ice cubes? Let's go somewhere else."

In the second basement bar, we sat on a two personal couch, I leaned on the far left, my eyes on the other tables. He stretched out his left arm on the back of the couch behind me. I tilted my body forward away from the back. The space was dim, music low, not much was happening. "Had enough?" "Yes." He drove me home, stepped out of the car, let me out of the passenger seat, watched me entered the house and drove off.

As I undressed that night, I was heightened with curiosity, thinking, "He's definitely not my boyfriend type, but seems straight forward and not pushy. Definitely the most interesting guy I've met so far." I figured as long as I kept my pants on, dates are great ways to know different types of people.

Beauti-asians

Sunday, I was at the Singaporean frat-house with the beauti-asians in Fitchburg, a short drive from campus. Someone was grilling barbeque ribs on the deck.

Of all the guys there, I was most comfortable with Troy, one of the handsome Singaporeans. He was friendly with both me and the Thai beauty. We had all gone dancing weekends before at a student organized party on campus. "Dance clubs are to be avoided." "The drunks tend to pick fights, especially with a bunch of Asian guys." Thai was absolutely stunning at the dance in a white dress, three inch heels, dark eye shadow and red lipsticks. I could do some simple makeup by then, thanks to a Mary Kay student representative in my Witte Hall days, and had a few pairs of going out shoes, but no high heels. One day Troy came with me to my one room apartment when I needed to pick up a check. When he entered the room, I noticed his face visibly changed when he saw how small it was, and at the orange brown shag carpet. The room probably smelled like curry chicken, which I cooked the night before with potatoes, soy sauce and curry powder. I had loved my room being cozy and with character, but compared to his modern and sleek four bedroom frat-house in a new apartment complex, mine became all of a sudden low class. It wasn't my look, but my shabby place that made me concerned. By then I had also learned that in the beauti-asians crowd, which had about ten core and another ten floaters, people do pair up and become couples, but it takes a long time of sizing and eyeing each other.

All that day, I wondered if Doug might call again.

You've got mail

Monday afternoon, I was again in the EE lab working on my program. Doug was there, but he didn't come by. I focused on my program. "One date is still better than no date," I told myself. When I finished and was about to leave, he came over.

"Did you check your email?"

"I haven't used email."

"Just login and type 'mail.'" Then he left.

I opened his email. "I thought of you before I went to sleep. I thought of you the minute I woke up..." My heart pounded. I couldn't read it there. At the printer, I tore off the perforated white and green computer paper. It was more than half sheet full.

Second date

Our second date was at a Chinese restaurant in dim light over Kung Pao Chicken, Hot Sour Soup, Ma Po Tofu and a vegetable dish.

After a few bites, he got up and went behind the wall of our two person table to blow his nose. "Excuse me. The chicken is spicy."

"Where did you learned to use chopsticks? I've not met any alien, hmm, westerner who can use chopsticks."

"I used to wait tables at a Chinese restaurant."

"A Chinese restaurant?"

"There was nothing else. I needed money. You know how I got the job? I went to the only Chinese restaurant in town. They told me they didn't need help. I convinced them they should have a waiter who could speak English." "By the way what is your Chinese name?"

"I don't like the sound of my Chinese name."

"Tell me."

"Hiu-ha, It sounds like hoo ha, doesn't it?"

"Hiu Ha?"

"Yes."

"It doesn't sound like hoo ha. I'm going to call you Hiu-ha."

I picked up a peanut with my chopsticks. Doug dropped his a few times. "Ha, got it."

"How do you like Math?"

"I have to pick something just to graduate. My original major was paper science. They don't have it here." I picked up another peanut. "Madison's very competitive. High school was easy." "I didn't have to work hard to get A's. I got one B. I was so mad at myself, I punched a hole in the wall."

The chicken was all gone. There was a tofu cube and a few chestnut slices left.

"How about you take the tofu? I'll finish the vegetables."

The plates were practically licked clean.

"It's my turn to pay." I snapped down my credit card.

"You have a credit card?"

"It's my parents'."

The eyes of a motherly Chinese waitress followed us all the way out the door.

In the Buick, he leaned over and kissed me once, softly on my lips. Then he started the car and dropped me home at the curb.

The next night, I was sitting at my six-person-dining-table-turned-desk in my room, my books and notebooks scattered about. My mind, well actually all my senses, were on Doug. Then I heard a whistle out of my window down on the street. I leaned over my desk to look out and there was Doug looking up and pointing his index finger upward. I nodded. He came in and we stood next to my table. "You doing your homework?" "Yes." He leaned over toward my notebooks. Next I know, our lips were sealed. His hand slid up my sweatshirt. My hand down to his jeans.

Halloween

Halloween, Doug told me he had a costume. I didn't but would go walk around with the beauti-asians. "Have to leave before ten, before this place goes crazy," Tenia said. I was a senior yet had not been to the State Street Halloween. Neither Ken or Bei were of the type to go to a "drunken orgy." The beauti-asians were at least cool enough to check it out. The State Street Halloween party was nationally known for its unique show of outrageous costumes, rowdiness, drunkenness, nudity and, some years, broken shop windows; but it was generally tame before mid-night.

"Hey Hiu Ha!" Doug was the Incredible Hulk, his whole body painted in green.

"Who's that?" There were about seven of us beauti-asians walking together.

"Who?"

"He was looking at you."

Before that, I had already seen a picture of Doug's body. It was his Mr. Teenage Wisconsin winning pose. In it he was standing on some green lawn in bright sunlight next to a five feet tall gold frame trophy. His lips pressed together and stretched into a huge grin. On him was nothing but a sliver blue brief. His arms and chest flexed to show off the muscle definition.

"You can keep it," Doug said.

Instead of saying, "Wow, you won the Mr. Teenage Wisconsin Bodybuilding contest? You look great," and then ask and listen to his explanation of muscle definition, symmetry, the art of posing for the judges, the hard work of dieting, weight lifting, and even tanning, as I would have if it were a gymnastics competition, I shoved the photo away inside my textbook.

Other times, when I strolled with Doug near the Hoofer Boathouse on Lakeshore Path, with him wearing a sleeveless fitted t-shirt and cut-off jeans, his body deeply tanned and in competition shape, and heads were turned, I wish then my friends would see me and say, "Who's that?" I could then say, "My boyfriend."

November 6, 1985

Dear Baba, Mama,

Sorry it's been a long time since I wrote last. Only one excuse: busy. Not just busy with homework. Because I'm about to graduate, my courses are more project orientated, which means I need to spend time to do research, discuss with classmates, etc. This kind of work is mentally tiring. Also since Bei isn't here anymore, I won't settle for being lonely, and there are many boys (Chinese boys) who like to ask me to join their activities, so most of the time when there are events I would go along. These friends are mostly acquaintances, not boyfriends. I can have a nice conversation with a few of them, but I'm keeping a friends-only distance. But lately there is an American boy who has been asking me out. He is not like a typical American, easier going than Bei, but still very serious about school. We see each other quite a lot, almost like boyfriend girlfriend. But I think we won't last very long. I feel I should get to know different types of people. You may worry I'll be taken advantage or something, but along this you don't need to worry. I know how to take care of myself. Wisconsin is relatively conservative. The Americans here are also more conservative than California or New York.

I'm still applying for grad school while at the same time looking for jobs. I took the GRE on October 12. I didn't do very well. There are a lot of English vocabulary I didn't know. When the result comes out, I'll let you know.

Everything well at home? Thank you for the birthday card. Tomorrow is my birthday, but still have to go to class and hurry on with homework, so won't really celebrate. This weekend my friends will celebrate with me. Bei and I rarely call each other recently. Looks like we will be done naturally.

All for now. You all have not been writing much either. No news means good news? Mama's work no problems? How about Baba? Please send Aunt Shan my regards.

Wish work makes you happy, live in peace and well.

Respectfully,

your daughter Hiu-ha

November 6, 1985

Fun and games

For my birthday, Doug got me a hamster in a cage. "She'll keep you company, better than your stuffed animals." I loved cuddling her furry body. But then in about a week when I got home, she was gone. I couldn't find her. "She ran off." I told Doug.

On my birthday weekend, I finally introduced Doug to the beauti-asians at the frat-house. I was nervous. Doug was at ease and charming.

"How did you two meet?"

"Hiu-ha needed help in the EE lab."

"Hiu-ha?"

"My Chinese name. He calls me Hiu-ha sometimes."

Everyone enjoyed him. We filled up with pork ribs.

Afterwards, my friends told me, "He's really good looking." Doug told me, "Your friends' place is nice."

Doug's place was on the west side of Madison, a bus ride or a long bike ride from campus. Doug usually kept his Buick parked at home. Our first ride from campus to his place, I was on my narrow wheel drop handlebar used bike, he was on a wide tire cruiser. On the first hill, I felt like I was starting to slide backwards. "Come on. We're almost at the top." By that time I had gotten quite good at riding my bike, could even go hands-off on straight roads. But my endurance, or lack there of, was trained only by wind resistance on the way from my house on Adam Street to the tennis courts near Picnic Point, never on hills, never learned to shift gear.

Doug loved his bike and loved riding. One of my favorite game was for us to ride pass each other and kiss on the lips. "Oops you miss again." "Have to lean farther out. You're not going to fall down." Another favorite was for him to pick me up in front of the Engineering

Building. "You wanna ride?" I'd then sit on the handlebar with legs dangling aside. He later added a pair of "stands" on his back wheel hub so I could actually get a ride standing up behind him.

His "room" took up the entire basement of their house. He had a few pieces of real furniture - a waterbed and some second hand night stands. He was particularly fond of his moss green Lazy-boy. "I had to fight my brother for it." It looked fitting in that windowless basement. The desk and shelves he built with plywood. The shower, he "rigged up" with a curtain hung on a circular metal bar around a hose mounted on the wall. Toilet was upstairs shared with his two housemates.

I knew one of his housemates better than the other. He was the one who convinced me to try cocaine. Roomy laid the powder in narrow stripes on the glass top coffee table. I only tried once, my nose was very uncomfortable, to say the least. "I don't like it either," Doug said. More so because Doug was constantly in training or at least maintaining his body for the next competition. He was extremely health conscious. His typical diet was something like six egg-whites for breakfast, steamed boneless chicken breasts and vegetables with Mrs. Dash for salt. I would still eat at McDonald's. "Don't eat that crap. It'll kill you." Because I was too thin according to my mom, I would eat anything, but Doug didn't want to get fat. "Dad once had a heart attack. He was in his thirties."

Roomy was a big help when we went club hoping. Because every other night at the dance clubs, Doug would get into a fight. Roomy and I became partners in pulling Doug off of people. "You piece of shit white ass," Doug would shout as we shove him out the club door. Once the fight started before we even got through the door when the bouncer asked for my ID. I was starting to think he had to fight for me when someone took a look at me which Doug considered disrespectful.

He did shield me. "You're the most beautiful woman in this club," he said when I wore my no-name black jersey dress of my English sherry party days. By then I was pairing it with low top black suede boots in three inch heels. We had gone out, got drunk, I stayed at his place overnight, slept late and then took the bus back to school the next morning. That same day, I left my purse at the bus stop, but someone delivered it to my house.

"Thank you so much! How did you find me?"

"Your address is on the student ID."

"Oh."

Not all were as helpful. One time Doug, his older brother Jeff and I were drinking in the middle of some park. I was drunk and my bladder was bursting.

"Just go pee on the grass by those bushes."

That was what they did, but I couldn't bring myself to it. "I jus go over dere and ask if I kin use dar toilet."

"You can try," they both laughed.

I went over to the house and knocked. "Maay I use yoo bath room? I nee to go ba lay."

"Piss off! You good for nothing drunks! Every weekend you leave nothing but trash…" The man was old, and not very friendly.

I stumbled back to Doug and Jeff.

"How did it go?" Jeff said with a smirk. "When you drink with the big dogs, you have to piss on tall grass." That became his joke on me every time we went drinking together. Jeff was in ROTC. He used to say, "I just tell it like it is."

I managed to walk all the way to the Mermaid Car Wash off University Avenue to use their restroom.

November 11, 1985

Dear Baba, Mama,

This morning from the phone, I could tell you are very worry about me. I understand your worry is coming from caring hearts. Comparing to many people here, I am blessed. Our family, although not wealthy, I hardly feel lack. I never have to ask for money, you would automatically send it. With life lessons, you have been training me since I was young. So I often feel like I'm unique. Also people have praised me for my intellect, praise me for my opinions and views on people in general. For this reason, I hope you can give me the same respect.

Sending me overseas to study, you have never stop worrying. When I went to England, you worry I could not adapt, worry I would learned from bad examples. When I come to the US, you worry I would suffer heartbreaks, worry I study too hard, worry I would marry the wrong man, worry my body can't take the stress, worry I can't handle the pressure of school. Now you must be very sick with worry. But I really don't feel you have anything to worry about. It's true I'm very close with this boy (his name is Doug), but I haven't thought as far as marriage. I have said before I don't plan on getting married before I turn 28. Even thought I just pass my 23th birthday, I feel I'm still very young. I still have a lot to learn, a lot to experience. This is the reason I broke up with Bei. With him, my future is fixed. He wants to work hard, move up in the world. I can only be his companion to help him do battle. When he first left, I did miss him. But I quickly found mental support. I found a part-time job, I made new friends. All of a sudden I discovered without him, my life is more full. With him, it was the opposite. We studied all day.

Everyday you plan for my future, want me to marry a good man.

Once I married, would you really stop worrying? I have been away from home for six and a half years now. Even though according to you I only know one and understand half. I understand your experience is valuable, but I don't feel my experience is any less. You feel like without your plans, I cannot create my own future, but I know my ability to adapt is very high. I came to Madison by myself. I went to Berkeley by myself. I could handle all that easily. I'm not the same as Min. She has her strong points. But what makes her happy does not necessarily make me happy. She is happy with whatever she has, slowly moving forward. But I want to fly. I know the higher I fly the harder I fall, the more painful it is, but I still want to fly. Coming to the US, my circle is not as simple as you think. Most Chinese who come to study keep themself in a small circle. There is a Hong Kong group, there is a Singapore group. But the people I know now includes people from every country, and I can connect with them. On contrary when I was with Bei, I only knew Singaporeans.

Although no one knows what would happen in the future, but Doug is treating me very well. I have never forgotten I am a Chinese. I haven't done anything to please him. Plus he is the only one in Madison who calls me Hiu-ha not Shirley. As for Bei, I think we are done. But as I have said before, I'm still young, not in a hurry to find a husband. Most important for me is that you don't worry about me. I know the road ahead is not smooth, but I have confidence. No matter what the problems may be, I can overcome. Don't expect I would be the main character of some sad Cantonese soap opera. I'm not as weak as you think, in need of protection. As for you thinking I can't endure loneliness, it may be true. But having one or two boyfriend doesn't make me a loose girl. Over here, regardless of Chinese or American, most have many boyfriends. I hope you don't try to make me into the perfect daughter you desire. I don't want to disappoint you. My expectation of myself is not necessarily lower than you of me. I'm also chasing the perfection in my heart. As for my future, I have my own plans. I hope whatever I do, you would support me (I'm not talking about financial support, but mental support).

Won't write more. Still have a lot of homework due. This semester's courses not easy.

Wish all safe and well.

Your daughter respectively,

Hiu-ha

November 11, 1985

Shirley Chau-Zarecki

Middle child

A week before Thanksgiving, Doug asked me, "You want to come with me to my parents' for Thanksgiving?"

I said yes thinking it would be like going to the Higgins.

"My dad is kind of racist. He might call you a chink. But he's harmless. It's just he's never met a Chinese."

I was not too concerned.

"If you get uncomfortable, we can leaving anytime. I'm not that close to my parents."

"Why not?"

"Well, for starters, I was a surprise baby."

I must have looked puzzled. Slowly it trickled out. "They couldn't afford the time or money for two boys ten months apart." "My parents don't believe in birth control. They are hardcore Catholics." "Dad wouldn't let Mom work outside of home. It's the Catholic tradition you know." "Then my brother Don came along.

"One winter my mom bought a pair of used girl's boots because it was dirt cheap. 'It's not girls boots,' she insisted. When I got to school, the boys laughed at me.

"One time I wanted an extra helping of mushrooms. My dad dump all of it on my plate. 'Here, eat it all,' he said."

Thanksgiving

Doug's parents' house was a pale yellow one-level on a quiet street among other modest ramblers in Central Wisconsin. Doug parked the Buick on the driveway and we entered through the two car garage. A big white sheepdog came and sniffed me. "She's tame. She's Lil's dog." The dog followed us to the back door. "She stays outside. My mom doesn't like dogs."

When Doug pushed the door open, I was hit with a "hi hi hi!" in a high shrill voice. A small woman with dark curly hair wrapped her long arms around me, then around Doug. "Hi mom." Behind her was what seemed like a mass of people in a small space. "Come on in. Hang your coats." Doug gave everyone hugs. I stepped inside and low waved to Jeff. A dense scent of turkey, butter and apple cinnamon filled the carefully decorated low ceiling kitchen, which opened to the dining room, which opened to the living room; all the furniture arranged neatly, walls lined with photo frames and country themed art work. On the dining table, a center piece of artificial flowers and fruits were surrounded by place settings in the fall colors of yellow, orange and brown. Doug introduced me to his other two brothers and his baby sister, who he had told me about fondly. "Hi." She was only thirteen, the prettiest little girl I had yet seen up close. Doug's dad said "Hi" curtly. I was slightly intimated.

"Shirley can put her bag in Lil's room. You can put yours downstairs," Doug's mom told Doug.

"She can go downstairs with me."

"Not in the same room."

"No mom, I'll sleep on the couch."

We went downstairs.

"How're you doing?"

"A bit overwhelming."

Bodybuilding trophies took up a corner of the basement. "Wow, you have a lot of trophies."

"Yea, I don't have room at my place. Mom said keep them here. She's my biggest fan." "Let me show you the yard."

Doug's dad was outside. "Dad, can we ride the four wheeler?"

"Go ahead." Doug wheeled the four wheeler out. Dad reminded Doug on how to start it the right way. Doug got on and motioned me to sit next to him. We zipped around the house. Lil and the youngest brother came out to watch.

"Here, you drive it," Doug told me.

I didn't know how to drive. "I don't know."

"It's easy. I can even drive it," Lil said.

Doug's dad appeared relaxed. I got on. Doug started it, and slowly I went, and then faster. I did a loop and got off smiling. "See it's easy."

We went back inside for the big dinner. All eight of us crowded around the oblong table, with folding chairs added because of me. If my house was lively, this was up a few more notches. Dad carved the turkey. We loaded up our plates. Mom lead the prayer. Then we ate. I didn't have to talk, just had to eat. Everyone else talked.

After dinner, I learned to play cards. "You know how to play cards?" I nodded. "You know UNO?" I shook my head. Once they explained, I understood it was similar to the card games I played all summer long with Min and Fai. They played other games and kept scores with pencil and paper. That night, Doug snugged into my room in the basement.

Next morning, Jeff, Doug and I were outside looking at a motorcycle. "Can I give Shirley a ride on it?" Doug asked Jeff. Jeff had taken a bad spill on it once. "It's safe," Doug told me. I hopped on behind Doug. It was a thrill I had always wanted, having admired bad boy motorcycle riders in Hong Kong. Now I was on one. Doug rode fast and showed off.

Sometime that weekend, I met Doug's huge extended family in a bigger version of Doug's parents' house. We had more food - turkey sandwiches, chips and sour cream dip, sloppy Joe, cheese and crackers, and of course marshmallow jelly. There were cans of soda and plenty of punch. The guys drank beer and played cards. "Holy crap." "Get me more quarters, hon." "Ah you cheat." Laughs and laughs. A few young nieces came said "hi." Doug introduced me to Grandma and Grandpa, the two people he was most fond of. Grandma was smily and soft spoken, "helloo," she held my hands. Grandpa wore a farm cap and looked just like Dad with a hidden smile and a curt hello. "They live on a farm. Someday I might get a part of it," Doug told me.

Later, Doug and I drove to Grandpa and Grandma's farm. Grandpa, Dad, uncles and brothers went deer hunting. Doug borrowed a rifle from Grandpa and taught me to target shoot.

"Mind the recoil."

"Woo." It was a hard recoil. I missed the beer can on the fence by yards.

"Move closer." I missed by a few feet. After a few more tries, I gave up.

When it was time to go, Doug warned me, "The goodbyes can take a long time, so when I say let's go, just get in the car." We drove off with Mom's face still inches away from the driver side window. "Bye bye bye!"

After a long silence, Doug said, "How was it?"

I was still trying to recover from the over-stimulation. "It was, hm," "good."

"Mom was easy on you. She figured you're just another pass through."

"She mentioned Kris a few times. I'm just your rebounder."

"She'll do that."

"Your dad's not racist. My dad is much worse."

Christmas

That Christmas, I went home. Doug went to LA for a photo shoot. He needed the money to pay rent and tuition.

"My parents will tell me to stop seeing you." I told Doug, "so I can't call you."

"Okay. Send me a postcard." He didn't seem to mind.

There was no winning against my parents. They eventually wore me out. I managed to calm them down by telling them it would not last. "We definitely would not get married. We're complete opposites." They could tell I was serious, so eased off on me just a little. Then Doug phoned me long distance in Hong Kong. My parents' place had only one phone in the living room.

"What are you doing? Told you can't talk!"

"Je t'aime."

"Em Je t'aime aussi."

We exchanged a few more French phrases with my parents behind my back.

I don't remember how I got through the rest of the Christmas break.

At the Madison Regional Airport, a few yards from my exit gate, Doug was leaning against a post facing me, in his weathered suede tan color bomber jacket and faded jeans. I stepped out the jetway in a new ankle length soft tweed coat weaved in brown and gold, my neck wrapped with a supersize wool scarf in tri-tone stripes of silver, aqua and navy blue, my feet in a new pair of black combat boots. He remained where he was cooly, I walked into his arms. We went home to my room in the Victorian house.

True love

If life was a fairy tale, this story would end here with "and we lived happily ever after."

But life is not a fairy tale. Real life actually starts after we find that special someone. It is when true love is tested against these principals - "Love is patient, love is kind. It does not envy, it does not boast, it is not proud. It is not rude, it is not self-seeking, it is not easily angered, it keeps no record of wrongs. Love does not delight in evil but rejoices with the truth. It always protects, always trusts, always hopes, always perseveres. Love never fails," - some Bible verse framed in hearts, given to us by Doug's mom and hung in our bathroom.

5

First lies

I let Doug use my apartment when I was in Hong Kong that Christmas of 1985. Sometime after I returned, I discovered I was missing an envelope with a hundred dollar bill.

"Did you see a white envelope this size?"

"No."

"I can't find it. I'm sure it was on this shelf."

Doug shrugged. I never found it.

That semester we took the same Computer Graphics class. A week after class started, Doug sat me down, "I think I did use you as a rebounder." I said nothing. "I don't want to hurt you later. It may be best if we spilt now."

The next few weeks I missed him terribly, yet still had to pretend I didn't see him in class. My cozy room felt empty. I walked by his little den next to the EE lab, where he kept a crockpot, where we spent much time on the couch and other times eating stew. Now the door was locked. I could not smell any cooking. Somehow this time no tears came. "I never expect it to last. It's supposed to be a little adventure. Sooner or later it will have to end, might as well be now," I told myself. It was easy to rejoin the beauti-asians, back as a core member instead of a floater.

I told my parents we broke up. "I told you you don't have to worry," I said.

By Valentines Day, I had gotten over Doug sufficiently to consider giving him a card. My thought was, "It doesn't cost me anything, but he might be happy to get it." I couldn't settle on one card, so I got two. One was funny, the other suggestive. The day after Valentines Day, I heard a knock on my door. It was Doug. "I've missed you too." Just like that, we got back together. The rest of the semester we spent a lot of time in the Mechanical Lab, working together on our Computer Graphics programming assignment.

I didn't tell my parents Doug and I got back together. That was the beginning of a long string of lies I made up to hide our relationship from them. After the ordeal of the previous Christmas break at home, I didn't want to go through the fight with them even once more. Who knows, we could break up again, that was my reasoning.

When my parents came to visit me in the summer, it was their first time.

"Madison is messy. The roads have holes," Dad commented.

"It's not as neat and tidy as Stanford, that's for sure."

"You have a big mosquito bite on your neck." Mom squinted her eyes at my neck.

I turned away. "Yea, the mosquitos here are huge. I have bad reactions."

It was the first blatant lie I made to my parents. Other times, I simply told them only what they need to hear and want to hear. They were not around me to know the difference.

Fast forward

I graduated in the summer of 1986, but continued onto grad school in Wisconsin. Doug graduated the following winter and took a programming job in Madison. For the next two years we lived together most of the time, except for a short stretch when he worked at UW in Dodgeville. He let me take his car so I could drive there every weekend, along the way between Madison and Dodgeville, I remember fresh cut hay aroma mixed with pig farm stanch. Doug had taught me how to drive by then.

Min was accepted by Stanford University for a one year program in Environment Engineering in September of 1986.

One year before my graduation, I sent out 100 resumes to companies in the Bay Area, telling them I would be around if they were interested in interviewing me. I spent two weeks in Palo Alto with Min and went on interviews. A small diskette duplication company - Mountain Computer - made me an offer and helped me obtained my H1 Visa. I left Wisconsin one semester before graduation to take the job. Doug stayed in Dodgeville. As with Bei, I said goodbye in my heart, but we told each other to stay in touch.

Mountain Computer was in Scotts Valley, a short drive north of Santa Cruz. Coincidently Troy and a few beauti-asians were also in the Bay Area. Their circle had shrunk then grew with new young professionals. I rejoined them.

Six months later, Doug quit his job, packed up everything and moved to the Bay Area. We moved in together to an apartment in Campbell. He found work writing software for a firm in Redwood City. Our friend circle grew to include many Americans besides the beauti-asians. Doug and I settled into an enviable lifestyle with our social circle and our jobs - we worked hard and played harder - volley balled on the Santa Cruz beach, backpack hiked the Yosemite State Park, skied the Sierra Mountains at Lake Tahoe, barbecued on weekends with friends, cheered the 49ers to Super Bowl. I remember freshly grilled abalone. The beauti-asians scuba dived for them which we roasted and ate right on the beach.

A snapshot

A snapshot. Oyster shots.

His name was John. Big John who introduced us to oyster shots. Big John knew all the good things in life. He drove a BMW. "It's the only car I'd drive," he told us. "It is the most responsive thing. I touched the wheel, and she turns, not too much, not too little, exactly as I want. I touch the gas pedal, she accelerates the exact amount."

Doug had been in his car and explained, "He drives like a mad man. But he's right. The car weaves in and out of traffic smooth as water."

When we were at the Giant's baseball game, John had his little sheets of paper and pencil. "Giants is the only team I've ever watched and ever will watch." He filled out the runs, strikes, hits and god knows what else in this sheet. I had never liked baseball. To me it was like watching grass grow. But Big John almost got me to like it. "There are reasons and mysteries in every detail of the game. You only have to capture it in these little sheet of paper."

Right, oyster shots. Doug and I both frowned at the slimy thing. "We drink this raw?"

"Yes, just let it slide down your throat."

I did. I was drinking thick saucy vodka. The oyster added a new dimension of sense and flavor. It was sensual. We downed one after another.

At some point, Doug and I crawled into our car.

"Can't drive. Can you?" Doug asked me.

"No."

We lay on top of each other somewhere in the back set. If we had sex, I don't remember. But I do remember waking up at 3 AM in the empty parking lot in our Toyota Supra.

The wedding

In 1988, I was turning twenty eight, Doug twenty seven. One day I told him, "I think it's time to shit or get off the pot," as Doug's brother Jeff might say. We talked it over and agreed we should get married. I finally told my parents about Doug and I. They recognized it was too late to object.

Doug proposed on Christmas Eve. He knelt down in the basement of his parents' house and handed me the ring. "Will you marry me?" "Yes."

We went upstairs and told everyone. "Let me look at this big beautiful ring. It must have cost you a fortune!" Doug's mom said. I went around showing everyone my ring.

In the car on our way to the Madison airport, Doug said, "The ring is cubic zirconia, not diamond you know." "What! Why didn't you tell me earlier? There I went around showing everyone, even your relatives. They all thought it was real diamond." The ring tinted my heart. Granted I had told Doug I just wanted a knot on our hearts with a string around our fingers to represent it. He compromised with a glass ring. Doug didn't explain, but now I think he didn't want to hear his mom saying, "How can you not have an engagement ring?"

I wanted a quick simple wedding, "Let's just get married in Las Vegas. Save the hassle and money for a nice honeymoon." Doug's mom insisted on a proper church wedding.

July of 1989, we flew back to Wisconsin. Doug's mom planned and arranged everything. Doug and I only picked out the dresses and designed the invitation. My dress was of the puffy princess style made with affordable rayon, in my hand was a bouquet of plastic flowers beautifully arranged by Doug's mom. The ceremony was in a tiny one room stippled white country church, one I insisted and got my way. "I think I finally got the one you want." Doug's mom found it standing alone on a country road somewhere near nowhere Rudolph. "It's perfect!"

My whole family flew in. Min and Tenia, Lil and Doug's sister-in-law were my bridesmaids. My brother Fai was one of the groomsmen along with the rest of Doug's three brothers. Fai stuck out a foot taller than the rest of the wedding party. Troy flew in from the Bay Area. He and the Taiwanesse beauty, the Singaporean beauty and her boyfriend and Tenia's boyfriend were my Asian representatives. The ceremony was long. We sweated bullets. It was late July with no air-conditioning. Doug talked gibberish to me as the priest went on. Finally "you may kiss the bride." When we went outside to the fresh air, Doug said, "I got myself a wife!"

During the wedding banquet at a country club, the groomsmen stole me, in my puffy wedding dress, to bars after bars to get me drunk. Fai watched me downed drinks and drinks in awed horror.

"It's the tradition to get the bride drunk, if we can," Jeff explained to Fai.

I got drunk. "I am a li, li, two dog." I hung myself over the back of a lounge chair in the ladies room. Doug was in no better shape. The bridesmaids were useless as far as getting Doug drunk, so the groomsmen took over after they were done with me.

Aunti fixed me with 7-ups. "It's the biggest day of your life. You can't go through it drunk."

By the time dances started, we were sober again. We had invited around a hundred guests but two hundred showed up for the dance. Doug pulled the garter-belt off my thigh with his teeth and tossed it to the gentlemen. I threw my plastic bouquet to the ladies. The men paid money to dance with me, as the ladies with Doug. My mom and dad even participated in the father daughter mother son dance. Dad surprised me with his popularity. Every time I looked his way, he was talking or laughing with a group of people around him, with Mom by his side, Min and my Asian friends close by. I noticed Fai hung around Lil, who was not so little anymore. We two-step Polka'ed until midnight.

My parents and Doug's parents got along well enough to exchange addresses to stay in touch. When Doug's dad became curious about my dad's Nikon, "Is this the latest model?" Dad gave it to him, "Here take it. I can easily buy another one." He had also provided the down payment for our condo in Cupertino as a wedding gift.

In hind sight, I'm glad Doug's mom insisted on a proper wedding, or I would not have this beautiful memory.

Soon I put away my glass engagement ring and wore only the gold band.

"Why don't you wear your big beautiful diamond ring?" Doug's mom would ask every other time she saw me.

"It's too big and it catches the threads in my sweaters," I told her. "Besides I might lose it or it can get stolen," "I don't like wearing jewelry, they are uncomfortable." These were some of my lies.

Our honeymoon was a short drive north to Napa Valley. There our souls renewed in the gentle hills, the fresh green vineyards, the wineries and wine tasting rooms at Beringer, Stag's Leap, Inglenook, Castello di Amorosa, and brought home bottles of Mondavi and Chateau Montelena.

Even though we had lived together on and off for three years, the marriage did give us a new level of intimacy. It wasn't just a checkmark on my resume.

First pregnancy

"Let's have a baby," Doug said out of the blue.

"I don't want any children right now. I'm not sure I want any children. " I had just finished my graduate classes, after a semester of night school at UC Santa Clara followed by completion of my research thesis between work. Wisconsin allowed all to transfer back and granted me my masters degree. I was tired.

"Don't you want to see what our children would look like?"

He planted a curiosity in me. I could not resist. I was almost twenty nine by then. It was approaching "now or never."

As soon as I stopped the pill, I got pregnant. Doug was elated. I was happy for him. The first months of pregnancy progressed smoothly. I craved authentic Shanghai noodles. "It is one thing we can't get here." "How about ice cream?" We put in baby curtains, bought a crib, painted the wall, gave away our parakeet to one of our beauti-asians friends. Our parakeet, "to replace the hamster that ran away," had grown accustomed to us. She could nibble food off our fingers, flew and land on our shoulders. But whenever she ruffled her feathers, fine dust scattered all over our carpeted living room. So she had to go. Clean air for our baby. In the last month I was gaining pounds a week, thanks to the beauti-asians who hosted hot-pot every other weekend. One can easily lose track of the amount of food one eats in a hot-pot party. Our host had bought a house with a long dining table, where two flaming pots could run simultaneously.

September 23, 1990

Dear Ba, Ma,

You may be surprised to receive my letter. I know I haven't written for a long time. Very lazy. Every time I sit down to write, there is always something else needed to be done, in the end I don't write anything.

I've been pregnant three months now. Stomach is not very big, gained six pounds, no nausea. Yesterday we went to see the doctor. He used the stethoscope (with amplifier), can already hear the fetus heart beat. My company's maternity leave has ten weeks, four weeks before and six weeks after. I want to return to my company to work part-time. Doug can work in the morning from 6 AM to 2 PM, I can work in the afternoon from 1 to 7 PM, find someone to watch the baby in the middle of the day, should be able to manage.

Few months ago I sent resume to Microsoft, two weeks ago they ask me to interview. Last week they verbally gave me an offer. It is in the international group, help them develop Chinese version of Windows. The job is very interesting, but they don't know I am pregnant. When I talked to the people in the group, I know the work is very tiring. Most of the time on the weekends, they have to go in to work. They stay at work very late on weekdays also. Plus Doug does not yet have a job offer in Seattle. So now I have decided not to take the job. I can contact them again after the baby is born. Maybe they will give me another offer.

Doug is studying MBA at Santa Clara, very busy. They just start classes, already a lot of homework. This course finishes in December. Hope he rests next semester.

Min goes to Bible Study every weekend, plus church, she is also very busy. She said Bible Study has a lot of social opportunity. I know she has been dating, but no one serious. I have also introduced guys to her, but she has not found anyone she likes. Actually she is still young, you don't have to worry. My friends in Hong Kong are also not married except one.

Don't know if Fai has moved this semester. I got his postcard from Germany. He didn't say where he would be next semester. If you have his new address or phone number, please send next time.

Still have not connected with Watson's sister. I don't have her phone number. She also has not phone me. Mom you don't need to worry. Doug and I won't share other people's private business. Okay, until next time!

Respectfully,
Hiu-ha, Doug,
September 23, 1990

Nataja

Doug and I decided Bay Area was too expensive for us with a baby. While we searched for jobs in Seattle, Min looked in Hong Kong. Hong Kong was experiencing an exodus of talents ahead of the 1997 turn over to China. Jobs previously unattainable had opened. Min already had a green card, so she decided to join the reverse flow.

I worked all the way up to the last week before my due date. I was healthy, so why not? Everything was ready, except childcare, we were picky. We had no family nearby but Min and the beauti-asians who were all busy professionals. I was getting stressed out.

The week before my due date, I took my maternity leave, but carried my big tummy around town interviewing home based childcare providers. Coming home after such a visit, I plopped down on the recliner, hot and exhausted. Doug was still at work. In the stillness of the living room of our condo, I realized suddenly I had not felt a kick for a while, but could not remember for how long. I waited for a kick, none came. I was not worried yet and waited another few minutes, still nothing. I called Doug. "She's probably just laying in a different position," Doug said. He came home. By then we were concerned. We called our gynecologist. Dr. Montgomery said, "Come in on the double." It was already dark. We drove to the Good Samaritan hospital. Doug glanced over at me. "Still nothing?" I shook my head. We remained quiet. Dr. met us in the delivery room. He and the nurse wheeled in equipment. Doug remained by my side. We had gone through Lamaze classes so Doug was trained.

"I'm very sorry, I'm afraid the baby is no longer alive," Dr. Montgomery broke the news.

"How can this be?" "Are you sure?" Doug started. "She was fine and moving this morning."

"Now what?"

"She still has to go through the delivery." "But she can use epidural or anesthesia if she wants."

I had been more than nervous about the delivery before this happened. I still have to go through the painful delivery? "Can I have C-section?" I finally spoke. I just wanted go to sleep on the hospital bed and wake up with the problem gone.

"C-section takes longer to recover. The scar might affect your next child birth. I don't recommend it. Anesthesia is effective. We can give you as much as you need since we don't have to worry about the fetus now."

Doug discussed it over with Dr. "We'll need you to be awake enough to push, put Dr. said he can use forceps to help retrieve the fetus."

We went through the procedure. "Nataja is beautiful." Nataja was the name we had planned. Doug held her and put her little fingers around his big index finger. Her eyes were closed, face peaceful but a little blue, her body also blue and bruised. I didn't want to touch her. Dr. Montgomery and the nurses encouraged me. "Hold her as much as you can now, otherwise you might regret it." They left Doug and I in the room to spend some time with her. "It's all right," Doug urged. I finally held her.

The next few days, we had to tell our parents, arrange for the funeral and find burial site. Heavenly Gates, a Catholic based cemetery in the foothills of Saratoga gave us a beautiful site at a cheap price, as long as we were Catholic. We said we were. We had attended Catholic marriage classes, which we felt qualified us. The cemetery was in a park setting a short ten minutes drive from our Cupertino condo.

At home, I had bursts of non-stop crying. It got to a point when Doug held me and said, "You have to stop crying. I don't know how to help." At night I still felt kicks. "It's just gas." I avoided looking into the baby's room. Doug's mom and Lil came to the funeral. I had wanted no visitors, but she would not take no for an answer. On the day, when the funeral director gave me private time to say goodbye, I had no more tears. I came out after just a minute. The four of us watched the small box lowered into the ground.

The autopsy did not review any information. The cord was not wrapped around her neck, even though her face was slightly blue suggesting possible suffocation. My dad thinks it may be Listeria, a bacteria in soft cheeses that shows no symptoms in the mother but can kill an unborn baby.

A week after the funeral, I was still on maternity leave. Doug said, "Troy is having a get together at his place. Do you want to try and go?"

"Okay." I put on a pale blue checkered dress which I thought covered my pregnancy fat well. On the drive over the hill to Scotts Valley, Doug said, "The dress makes you look kind of fat, you know."

"Stop the car!"

"Why, I'm just letting you know."

"Stop the car!"

Doug stopped. I got out. Doug came out. "I'm sorry. I was just making a comment." "I'm sorry." "You can't just stand here. How would you go home?"

"I don't care how. I'll hitch a ride. I'll walk."

"Come on. We can forget the party."

Eventually I got in the car, and we went home.

I started looking for escape. Paris. I had always wanted to go there and live for a few years after England. I could use my French, sit by a sidewalk cafe and sip coffee, buy fresh pastry on my way home. Doug had never been outside of the US. He was coming with. "You're not going without me," he said. I booked tickets and hotels, bought and studied Foder's and Frommer's travel books.

Doug and I went to Paris, sat outside for coffee, ate smoked salmon, slurped mushroom soup and sampled other gourmet food. "You can't find bad food here," someone told us. We then drove to Loire Valley, checked out the Chambord, visited a farm house, tasted a country stew of pheasant in red wine sauce. It was easily the best meal of my life. The trip healed me.

Doug and I did not attend any neonatal death support group, didn't buy or study any copping mechanisms. I took only one advice. I bought a box, wrapped it with decorative material, put an artsy design on its cover, and put in the photos we took of Nataja, along with all the condolence cards and letters, and the goodbye notes Doug and I wrote, tied the box with a ribbon and stored it under blankets on the top shelf of my wardrobe.

The next time when I joined Troy's Hawaiian themed party, I wore a bright flowery orange one-piece short and put a flower in my long hair. Everyone commented I was back to pre-pregnancy shape and looked even better.

I visited Nataja's grave often, sometimes with Doug, often by myself. The green grass, the warm sun, the gentle surrounding hills soothed me. During one such visit, I heard an unusual bird cry, it was as though telling me another baby was on the way. I shook out of my "stupa" and went home.

Parker

The pregnancy with Parker was a psychological challenge. Every step along the way, I wondered what I had done wrong with Nataja. "Should I not eat this? Not that?" I had not drunk wine or coffee with Nataja. "Shall I not go to hot-pot parties?" Dr. Montgomery encouraged us, "It was not in your control. There was nothing you could have done."

Doug and I continued searching for jobs outside of California, but instead of Seattle, we decided to try Minneapolis. I pictured in my mind a sunny backyard of lush green lawn. Meanwhile Min found a dream job with the Hong Kong Environmental Agency. "I'll go for at most two years, just to get the experience." She left me with her Honda Civic. "Sell it for me," she said.

In March of 1992, Parker was born a healthy 6.8 pound baby. Dr. Montgomery delivered him at the same Good Samaritan Hospital. He induced the birth a week early, "Just in case."

Once in a while, I would open the box I made in Nataja's memory, to read the cards, especially the one signed by everyone at my workplace, even by people I did not know. I avoided Nataja's photos, not wanting to look at pictures of a dead baby, even though she was my daughter. Gradually I opened the box less and less and then none at all, after I got busy with Parker.

Doug's mom still send cards or messages to remind me of her birth and death. I keep forgetting. I would however make a point of visiting her site whenever I am in the Bay Area, bringing fresh flowers, cleaning her in-ground stone and soak in the tranquil setting of the park.

April 26, 1992

Ba, Ma, Min,

How are you? We are very well. I started work on April 21. Everyday I work for five, six hours. In the morning at 11 o'clock, I take Parker to nanny's home. In the afternoon at 5, Doug goes to bring him home. Three more weeks and I will have used all my vacation. At that time, I have to work full time. We like Parker's nanny very much. She loves kids, has 14 years of experience. I saw how she takes care of a 7 year old girl, very healthy and happy, so feel quite confident to let her care for Parker. Parker is now ten pounds heavy, can smile. Every day can smile three to four times, can see people, turn his head, lift his head. At night at 10 o'clock after he has eaten, morning at 2 and 5 he will need to eat again. I feed him at 2 AM, Doug feeds him at 5 AM. My body has recovered, ten pounds heavier than before.

Doug has found a pretty good job in Minneapolis. The company does consulting work. The company hires him, then sends him off to other companies like 3M to do projects. The company also has interest to hire me, but needs to interview me before they can make a decision. This company is quite big in Minneapolis. Also they limit eight work hours per day, beyond that is overtime pay, so we are very interested. Next Wednesday he goes to interview.

I agree to move to Midwest not because Doug wants to go, but I feel our future in California is limited. Our biggest problem is no time, no money. With a child, these two problems become worse. We can work five more years still cannot afford this condo. But this condo is only big enough for now. When Parker grows bigger, he needs room to move around. If we add another child, there is not enough space for sure. Here in CA, we are lower middle class. In Minneapolis we will be upper middle class. Because in the Bay Area, there are many people of our skill level. Most are single or divorced or married with no children, so they can afford more time to work, can make more money. By comparison we would become less competitive. Midwest lifestyle is more layback, more stable, better suited to bring up children. Of course there are less Chinese there, weather is colder, but if Tenia and her family (our Madison old classmates) can live there happily, and I did not complain when in Madison, I will also like to live there. Attached is some news article that reflects the decline of the quality of life in California.

If we move, the biggest problem is this condo. If we sell it now, the most we can get is $220,000. We bought it for $215,000. So the gain of $5000 cannot even offset processing fees, then you and we would both lose money. I believe this condo after two or three years will increase in value. So if we wait, we can all make money. On the other hand, interest rate and home price is lower now, so it is a good time to buy. But with our savings we can't buy a house in Minneapolis and pay mortgage of this condo. Houses in Minneapolis is cheap. With $130,000 we can buy a very nice house already. Below is our proposal:

1. You give me $50,000. This condo we give to you. We find someone to rent it for you (we hire property manager), help you pay mortgage, homeowners fees and property tax, i.e. we help you share the expense of this condo. In the end, the condo is yours. With $50,000 we an buy a house we like, monthly mortgage would be cheaper. We will have enough money to help you pay the condo. Of course the condo needs to be rented, can't leave empty, otherwise we can't support it.

2. You give us $20,000. Condo is yours. You support it yourselves.

3. If you don't give us any money, we wait until the price goes up above $250,000, then sell it. You take $116,000. We take $134,000 (based on you paid $100,000 down payment) Meanwhile we rent a place in Minneapolis. Two years ago, a unit like ours sold for $245,000. We believe Bay Area real estate when rebound can sell for $250,000. I believe the longer we wait, the higher the price. In five or six years, it will worth $280,000 or more.

Minneapolis real estate value has also been rising. Over 5 years it has grown about 50%, so not a bad investment. This condo on the other hand has not a good investment so far. Over the last 3 years we have spent close to $60,000 (this includes improvements we made to the condo and property tax and homeowners dues). If we sell it today we make no money whatsoever.

* * *

Parker is growing very fast. Don't know when you will come visit him? We hope we can bring him home for Christmas.

Respectfully,
  Hiu-ha
  April 26, 1992

The break away

My parents almost disowned me after they read this letter. My mom's collection of my letters ended with this one.

For years, I could not understand why they were mad at me. I thought the terms were more than reasonable. I had forgotten my parents gave us the initial down payment for the condo to begin with. They could easily give us another one. They did not like my tone, completely void of emotions or love. But they blamed it all on Doug. They thought I was not capable of the economic analysis. I had never had any interest in economics.

For my parents and most Hongkongers, the Midwest was a place to pass through. The real opportunities were on the two coasts. We were in high tech, what could be better than working and living in Silicon Valley? It was like getting accepted to Stanford University and then quit. From my standpoint, Doug and I really wanted to move to Minneapolis for a standard of living we wanted, not for the glory of living in some famous area. But I knew my parents would not support our move. It was again living my life verse how they wanted me to live. This time, I could not just lie to them by telling them what they need to hear or want to hear. It was my way or no way.

Eventually my parents accepted our first proposal, also completely void of emotions.

We bought our dream home in a suburb of Minneapolis, a modest $170,000 three bedroom with lots of natural light, a large enough yard to throw a football, or let loose a dog.

Fai

In May of 1992, just two months after Parker was born. We moved to Minneapolis. Doug took the new job. I also found a job two month later with the company I would end up with for 26 years.

Sometime in June, Grandpa Cuan passed away. Before I had time to grieve, I received a phone call from Min a few weeks later. "Fai had a car accident. He is dead." I held the phone in my hand. "The funeral is in Bath next week. Can you come?" She told me Fai was in coma for a week. Dad was in Bath. Min was going to bring Mom to Bath from Hong Kong.

"Why didn't you tell me earlier? I could have seen him when he was still alive!"

"Why are you shouting at me? I have enough to deal with already. You have no idea what I'm going through, have to support Mom. All you can think of is yourself! The funeral is at E Hooper and Son. You can look it up." Then she hung up.

"I'm an uncle!" Fai's voice came through the phone.

"When are you coming to see Parker?"

"I'll come this summer, for sure."

Fai in his white bridegroom suit at my wedding, stood out from the crowd. Fai at our second wedding banquet in LA with Grandma Grandpa Cuan...

At some point Doug appeared next to me. I heaved into his chest.

"Fai is dead."

"What? No!" He held me while I sobbed.

I pulled myself away. "I need to book flights to Bath."

We went to the study. I sat at the desk, facing the window. I was looking at the grass outside, but not seeing it. I was in some kind of jelly, a medium that held me afloat, connecting me to the grass. I was vaguely aware of Doug at his desk, but he was not in the jelly. I shook out of the jelly, and made arrangements to fly to Bath, England.

I zoned out on the train from London to Bath.

"Big Sis, can you read me Ding Dong Cat?" Fai's hands holding a comic book.

"Again? Didn't we just read it yesterday?" But I sat down on the sofa, Fai cuddled next to me and I read.

"Sis, help!" Min ran out the hallway to the dinning table, Fai followed, fist in the air.

I raised my head briefly from my Heavenly Sword and the Dragon Saber. They circled around the table a few times and then Min disappeared to the servant's quarter. I went back to my book.

"Big Sis, where did Second Sis go?"

I knew Min liked to hide in the clothesline area behind the kitchen. "What will you give me?"

"Oh, never mind I know where she might be."

"Turn it off! Turn it off!" Fai said in a hushed tone. Min and I jumped off the sofa and switched off the TV, just in time before Mom and Dad came in the door. Dad walked to the TV and felt the warmth on its top. "Crap. Busted." Dad pulled the power cord off the TV taking it with him to his room.

"I'll be Fok Ching-tung and you be Chan Ka-lok ," I told Min, waving my plastic sword.

"What am I then?"

"Fai, you can be the bad guy and fight us."

"I don't want to be the bad guy again."

"Do you want to play or not?"

"Aaall-right."

"Don't you shoot," I said and stared down at Fai. Fai stared back holding the BB gun steady. "Don't you dare." I had nothing and was defenseless. I did not blink. Fai didn't either. Then he pulled the trigger. "You shot me!" I pounced on him and punched and punched. He was bigger than me by then and had a good layer of fat. He just let me punch, until tears streamed down my face…

Bath

From what we gathered. Fai was on holiday in Bath with three friends, all from Imperial College in London where Fai was studying for his masters degree in Computer Science. The car was a Susuki jeep, a cheap vehicle popular among students, with a trendy appearance, but the chassis was of light weight material and no strong support beams. Fai was sitting in the passenger side back seat. The driver moved right to pass (the English drive on the left side of the road), not realizing another car was coming fast. He swerved to the right but it was too late. The oncoming car hit Fai's side of the jeep. The boy sitting in front of Fai was killed instantly. The other two survived. Fai was rushed into the hospital but did not regain consciousness before he died. Dad said his hands and mouth moved while Dad was holding him before he passed away. Dad was the only one by his side. Mom was in LA taking care of Grandma after Grandpa Cuan died. Min got Mom to fly back to Hong Kong. She became the responsible adult to break the news to Mom making sure she would be stable, with help from a few doctor friends of my parents, who was ready with medical support.

In the end, we all made it to the funeral. A few of Fai's classmates also traveled there from London. Doug stayed home with Parker. We didn't tell the Higgins until months after the funeral.

I took the train to London, to Fai's apartment. An Indian girl about Fai's age gave me his remaining possessions. I took Fai's turntable and records. "It's a Linn. The best brand. Fai put a lot of time and money into it." "He doesn't like digital music. Thinks it distorts the sound. He thinks only analog sound is pure." I did not ask who she was or her relationship to Fai, but she talked in a dream like voice, eyes far away. I wrapped the turntable, the vinyl records, a notebook and a school magazine of which Fai was the chief editor. Somehow they all fit into my suitcase.

Back in Minneapolis, Doug and I converted the Linn's power supply to US standard. I listened to Fai's records. One sounded half French half New Orleans Jazz but I did not recognize the musician. Occasionally when I was driving or in the shower, tears flowed. But most of the time, I was too busy to grieve.

A journal entry

July 3, 1993

Now that I am a mother of a one-and-a-half year old, I have to write faster, much faster than when I was a college student. Time is so limited. I want to pick back up on writing because I want to collect some of my thoughts, or more correctly, give myself some time to have thoughts. I want to remember more of my childhood, especially times I spent with Fai.

The first time I saw Fai was in a picture. He looked so pretty I thought he was a girl. I thought my parents lied to me that I had a brother and a sister when in fact I had two sisters. I don't know for how long I actually believed that. Fai was a beautiful baby. He had big brown eyes and rosy cheeks. For some reason, Min and I always thought he was cuter when he was younger. When he was five, we thought he was cute at two or three. When he was ten, we thought he was cute at six or younger. We never gave him much respect, mostly because he was much younger than we were. I remember teasing him when he was over five years old and still wet his bed. He never got good grades in schools in Hong Kong. He never was much of an athlete. I could always wrestle him down (before he reached ten), but then I was sixteen when he was ten. We thought he was spoiled. He used to get more toys than us. He would get away with not having to do any housework when Min and I were assigned chores, like washing Dad's car.

Fai himself was very easy going. He would share his toys with me. He tried to do things we asked just to please us. I wish I had included him in more of our conversations and activities.

Travis

That was a year after Fai's death when I wrote about him in my journal. Then my grieve for him ceased.

One day, some time after Parker turned two, I sat watching him and felt a small emptiness. We had settled into some kind of routine. Work and home life kept me busy, but our house had become too quiet. "It's time to have another baby. Parker needs company." We decided.

About that time, China had opened up wide enough such that tourism became possible, so Doug and I planned a trip there as a last hurrah before two boys in diapers. Doug's mom offered to watch Parker. "Go enjoy Shirley's home country." I went off the pill and got pregnant just before our planned departure, so Travis the fetus came along for the ride to China, and survived the not yet sanitized cities like Xian. Doug barely made it through the culture shock, and I, E. coli. I lay feverish in bed in Hong Kong until Dr. Yuen, Dad's colleague and friend and Chair of Infectious Disease at HKU now responsible for Hong Kong's COVID 19 response, made a housecall and treated me back to health.

The trip to China made me decide to become a US citizen, not because of the E. coli, but because Doug's US passport was more convenient to travel to China than my China born Hong Kong resident passport, which was second rate to those born in Hong Kong. "Why is a China born native Chinese treated worse than a foreigner?" So in October of 1994, I took the oath and officially became a US citizen.

Six months later in April of 1995, a week before the due date, our doctor induced the birth as a precaution. Travis was born a big and healthy 8.3 pound baby. It was quite difficult to get him out.

6

Heavy burden

Doug and I never did have enough time or money. The burden of life
we put on ourselves slowly but surely weighted us down.

December 16, 2005

It was December of 2005, Parker was in middle school and Travis was in fifth grade. I had two glasses of red wine at the end of a terrible, horrible, no good, very bad week, and wrote -

It all started last Saturday. I decided to take this big box out of the back of the Expedition after it had been riding there for a week. The box was so big and heavy that I could not close the truck tailgate while holding the box. So I left it open and went inside the house. Once inside, I had a million other things to do. I never went back to close the tailgate. An hour later, Travis was late getting dressed for hockey. We had to be there at 10:40 AM and it WAS 10:40 AM. Travis was still not ready. We finally got out the door and into the Expedition. I backed out of the garage... with the tailgate open. I heard a crunch. The hatch door hit the top of the garage! From the rear window, I could see the top beam of the garage doorframe hanging half way down. Luckily the hatch door was only slightly scratched.

I spent the rest of the morning nailing the garage door beam back before rushing off to pickup Parker from gymnastics.

The rest of the week, I had to think about how to get the truck fixed.

Sunday evening, Doug could not find his key chain, which held the truck and ski rack keys. I was the last person to have used it. We looked in all the possible places, but could not find it. The truck key will cost us over $200 to replace!

The same evening, a bottle of red wine slipped out of Doug hand and broke. We spent the evening frantically cleaning up the scattered glass. The red wine ruined the carpet that was installed just two year ago. Meanwhile, dinner got cold.

Monday, Doug had his LASIK eye surgery. We had set aside money in the FSA account all year for this. Doug had been so busy that he could not get it done. Now that it is December, we risk losing the money all together. He finally made it to the surgery December 12th. He was practically blind for 4 hours after the surgery. I got him home and went back to work. Parker and Travis served him dinner and generally took care of him during that time.

Tuesday, we had the biggest snowfall of the year. I left work early in hopes of getting home in time to pick up Travis from DI (Destination Imagination). I ended up sitting in traffic for 2 hours, so I was 2 hours late. Thanks to Pam, the DI manager, who brought Travis home.

Wednesday morning, I didn't realize Bucky the beagle's invisible collar had been out of battery. When I let him out in the morning, I saw him cross the fence and head towards the backyard of our neighbor. I tried to call him back but he ignored me as usual. I was not dressed to trudge through deep snow to get him. Luckily some kids went to the bus stop early. They were more than happy to track down Bucky for me. When Travis finished breakfast, he joined them for the hunt. They got him back just minutes before the school bus arrived. This incident plus the hangover traffic from the snowstorm meant that I was late for work, again.

The same morning, Doug had to fire an employee. He had to stay at the studio in the evening to take over the duties of the fired trainer. I had to go home early to take care of the boys.

Sometime in the week I had to make up for the 2 hours of work I missed this day. Since my Friday was already booked, I had to make it up Thursday, on top of the 11 hours I had to work normally on Thursdays.

Thursday, I worked form 8 AM to 9 PM.

Before I head home from work, tired and still hungry from eating only a can of vending machine tuna salad, I found that the Audi was out of windshield fluid. With the salt and sand and slush from the snow, I could not see without the windshield washed. So I had to stop and fill the windshield fluid.

Doug and Travis, knowing I would be hungry, saved me a delicious bowl of beef and noodle from dinner. Great, as if I need more carbohydrate and red meat before bedtime after not exercising for a week, but I wolfed it down anyway. So what if I add a few more inches to my waist.

After I ate, they showed me the mess Bucky had made earlier in the day. He had had no exercise since Sunday and decided to tear up my Christmas decorations and spilled the glass of sand and seashells. I got to clean that up before going to bed. (Doug and Parker don't do Bucky work.)

Friday, my day off for the week, I got to sleep-in until 6:45 AM. I woke up Parker, made him breakfast as usual and sent him off to catch the school bus. Just as I was starting to wash up and get myself dressed for the day, Parker popped into the bedroom and announced that he missed the bus. I was upset about having to drive him to school, given that I had a full day ahead and really couldn't afford to spend extra time driving him, but I had no choice. I told Parker he had to pay a fine of $5 for my time. He argued that it was not his fault. I argued back. Then he said, "Everything you just said is wrong." I was stumped. How do you counter that? Finally I said, "I'll let you off this time, but next time it will cost you $10."

When we got close to the school, the road was completely packed with school bus and auto traffic. We weren't moving. It was 10 degrees below zero and all the good parents decided to drive their middle schoolers to school instead of having them walk or wait at the bus stop. I admired those parents; I however was there not by choice. The last thing I wanted to do was to sit in my car and wait the half hour to get to the school building. I turned into the adjacent high school parking lot and made Parker walk to school from there. I drove off as Parker, carrying his heavy backpack and saxophone, climbed the foot-deep snow covered hill toward the school. I felt awful as I passed the other parents patiently waiting in line to drop their kids right at the front step.

Meanwhile, Travis was alone at home and I needed to wake him up, feed him and send him off to catch the school bus. When I got home, Travis just got out of bed. He said to me "We have DI this morning at 8." I looked at the clock. It was 8:10! Never mind breakfast, I grabbed an energy bar for Travis and we headed out the door.

After I dropped off Travis, I had a little time to wash a load of laundry before my appointment with the chiropractor. As I dumped out the laundry, Bucky immediately started sniffing the dirty laundry pile. He got something and proceeded to roll in it. This could only mean he had found something disgusting. I ordered Bucky to back off and leave it alone. It looked dried and brown. I told Bucky to stay away, quickly went into the bathroom to get a tissue. It took all of about 2 seconds, but when I came back, the thing was gone. I looked at Bucky. He appears to have stayed where he was, but I know he had already swallowed it!

Meanwhile, I was running late for my first appointment with a chiropractor. I have had a nagging dull shoulder pain for a few years. I rushed out the door again, and was another 15 minutes late, and could have lost my appointment all together. That's the story of my life - running, running, late, late and late again.

In the afternoon, I finally made it to the YMCA for a workout. On the way out, I had my truck key and the YMCA membership card in my hand. I seem to remember putting the card in my pocket. When I got out of the truck at home, I dug into my pocket and the card was gone. I looked everywhere in the truck, it was not there. Somehow I had lost the card from the Y front door to the truck. I wanted to go back and look for it in the parking lot of the Y, but the boys are home waiting for me to take them to the dentist. I was again running late and couldn't possibly go back at that moment. After the appointment, it was dark and impossible to look for it. I tried anyway but could not find it. No one had turned it in either. Now it will cost me $15 plus 15 to 30 minutes of my time to replace it.

Today must have been the grand finale of my terrible horrible no good very bad week.

June 17, 2007

One of the scant entries in my notebook dated June 17, 2007 -

Over the course of 18 years, things settled into a way that neither of us are happy with, but we can no longer change. He has strong preferences for everything, and uses his will to get it his way, from how to stack dishes to what cars to buy. He usually isn't happy until he gets his way. I on the other hand don't feel strongly about very many things. My preference is usually whatever makes the most people happy. If everyone is happy, I'm happy. Now after all these years, when I start to have a preference and try to push for what I want, things can get ugly. The yard is one. I wanted sprinkler, he wanted more landscaping. We are deadlocked. Landscape requires weeding, pruning, mulching, none of which I enjoy doing. I don't mind mowing, but then he complains that I don't do any yard work. I wanted to put patio blocks down to create a walkway. I would have done it last weekend. But "not enough blocks," "what about..." In the end, enough cold water is poured over my head that I no longer want to do it. If I can't have the kind of yard I want, how does he expect me to want to do any work? I'm not a laborer who takes work directions. Speaking of directions, it's come down to I get to do what he tells me. I don't get to decide how or what to do. It would be such a tremendous freedom to live on my own and do what I want. Unfortunately, we can't separate right now. Our assets are so tied together it would take lawyers to separate. We don't have the time and money to do this. We don't even have enough money for me to move out. The boys will still require us to deal with each other; who drives who when; who attends which event. I don't see how separating would free myself from him; the only advantage is to allow me to date other people, which I have no interest whatsoever right now.

Cooking

The next page of my notebook -

Cooking.

When I don't cook, he complains.

When I do cook, he complains, "made a big mess, spent too much time in the kitchen." With all the shopping and cooking I did last night, the dinner was blah.

Father's Day.

Everyone's been working on the yard. I figured they will be hungry for lunch. Took a bowl of noodles to make salad. Doug walked in, looked at the bowl and growled, "You didn't take all my noodles, did you?" Here I was trying to make lunch for the whole family, instead of showing appreciation, he'd rather make his own lunch with "his noodles." Before he's even seen or tasted what I was about to make, he already disliked it. Yet everyday he complains, "Why don't you cook?" "When was the last meal you cooked?" In the end, all my noodle salad got eaten, yet no one complimented my dish.

Sometime in 2012

The next notebook entry was sometime in 2012 -

Before you lose your patience, raise your voice to scold me, do you stop and think you are thankful that, because of me, you get to go biking at the cabin on a weekday?

True love

…A whole shelf of glassware toppled on me. Every piece of glassware shattered into tiny pieces. Glass pieces on me and maybe even in my skin. People around me started to help pick up the pieces. The mess was so big it seemed impossible to clean it all up…

If it were up to me, I would have done nothing, and let the wind blow me wherever it takes me. Doug being Doug, decided for me.

During the last of the three free marriage counseling sessions, Doug's hand clutched a coffee cup and took sips of it throughout the session. I knew him well enough to know it wasn't coffee in the cup, but red wine. The purpose of the counseling sessions, as our counselor put it, was to "see if there's still any amber left to rekindle the fire." She turned to me and basically said I should divorce him. Doug's asshole facade worked, and I divorced him.

It is taking me a lifetime to learn about love.

There is a difference between love and attachment. An attachment is when I have to be physically with someone. It can be a husband, boyfriend or my children. With attachment, I cannot bear to lose that someone, and so I either change myself to suit that someone, or exert influence or control over them to keep them with me.

Love, I now know, is not like that. Love is unselfish. Love sets the other person free. Love allows the other person to achieve their potential, to live their life to the fullest. Love gives, but does not ask for anything back.

He set me free, no matter the cost, to himself.

So I flew.

Out of my thirteenth floor apartment window, a bouquet of colorful balloons, the kind you see in amusement parks where a child says, "mom, can I have a ballon" and she pays the man holding a bundle of strings to which a collection of balloons are tied, and the man says, "which color" and the child points and the mom gets him one; except this time, the whole bundle; the bundle of blue, yellow, red, white, purple, orange, green bubbles stuck together, cut loose, and floated from the west to the east and then upward and disappeared.

Made in the USA
Middletown, DE
23 January 2022

59455640R10099